INSIGHT'S
Bible Reading Guide
NEW TESTAMENT

FROM THE BIBLE-TEACHING MINISTRY OF
CHARLES R. SWINDOLL

INSIGHT FOR LIVING

INSIGHT'S BIBLE READING GUIDE: NEW TESTAMENT

From the Bible-Teaching Ministry of Charles R. Swindoll

Charles R. Swindoll has devoted his life to the clear, practical teaching and application of God's Word and His grace. A pastor at heart, Chuck has served as senior pastor to congregations in Texas, Massachusetts, and California. He currently pastors Stonebriar Community Church in Frisco, Texas, but Chuck's listening audience extends far beyond a local church body. As a leading program in Christian broadcasting, *Insight for Living* airs in major Christian radio markets around the world, reaching people groups in languages they can understand. Chuck's extensive writing ministry has also served the body of Christ worldwide and his leadership as president and now chancellor of Dallas Theological Seminary has helped prepare and equip a new generation for ministry. Chuck and Cynthia, his partner in life and ministry, have four grown children and ten grandchildren.

Published By: IFL Publishing House, A Division of Insight for Living,
Post Office Box 251007, Plano, Texas 75025-1007

Editor in Chief: Cynthia Swindoll, President, Insight for Living
Executive Vice President: Wayne Stiles, Th.M., D.Min., Dallas Theological Seminary
Writers:
John Adair, Th.M., Ph.D., Dallas Theological Seminary
Alicia Beaver, B.A., Journalism, Baylor University
Terry Boyle, Th.M., Ph.D., Dallas Theological Seminary
Jim Craft, M.A., English, Mississippi College
Kimberlee Hertzer, M.A., Christian Education, Dallas Theological Seminary
Bryce Klabunde, D.Min., Western Seminary
Brian Leicht, Th.M., Dallas Theological Seminary
Graham Lyons, M.Div., Columbia Biblical Seminary
Mike MacKrell, Th.M., Dallas Theological Seminary
Barb Peil, M.A., Christian Education, Dallas Theological Seminary
Wayne Stiles, Th.M., D.Min., Dallas Theological Seminary
Theological Editors: John Adair, Th.M., Ph.D., Dallas Theological Seminary
Derrick G. Jeter, Th.M., Dallas Theological Seminary
Content Editor: Amy L. Snedaker, B.A., English, Rhodes College
Copy Editors: Jim Craft, M.A., English, Mississippi College
Kathryn Merritt, M.A., English, Hardin-Simmons University
Project Coordinator, Creative Ministries: Melanie Munnell, M.A., Humanities,
The University of Texas at Dallas
Project Coordinator, Publishing: Melissa Cleghorn, B.A., University of North Texas
Proofreader: Paula McCoy, B.A., English, Texas A&M University-Commerce
Cover Designer: Margaret Gulliford, B.A., Graphic Design, Taylor University
Production Artist: Nancy Gustine, B.F.A., Advertising Art, University of North Texas
Cover Image: Ruins from the city of Ephesus; image by Wayne Stiles, Th.M., D.Min.,
Dallas Theological Seminary

ISBN: 978-1-57972-935-6
Printed in the United States of America

TABLE OF CONTENTS

A Note from Chuck Swindoll

Some things are givens.

One important "given" at Insight for Living Ministries is the confidence we have in the Bible. The regular exposure we get to God's Word through the work we do reminds us daily what a remarkable book the Bible is. And by remarkable, I mean *miraculous*. Along with being remarkable, the Bible is amazingly resilient. It has survived every critic, even the most outspoken. Opponents come and go, but God's Word lives on.

Yet in spite of Scripture's remarkable, miraculous, and resilient characteristics, amazingly few Christians are satisfied with their grip on it. It's not that they're embarrassed by the Bible. No, most claim to love it. But they are embarrassed to admit they're virtually ignorant of this Book for which they say they would die.

Years ago, I heard a story from a friend who gave entrance exams to new students at a Christian college. These kids had been raised in *Christian* churches; they were entering a *Christian* college. And on the exam, which was really just a questionnaire of basic biblical facts, was the question, "What are the Epistles?" One young man responded, "The Epistles are the wives of the apostles."

I found his reply so absolutely hilarious that I later shared it in church. Looking into the congregation, I noticed one young man not laughing. Afterward, he immediately came up and asked, "If they weren't the wives of the apostles, whose wives were they?"

And ours was a well-taught church!

No matter their home churches, most believers just aren't equipped with biblical facts. I know it isn't considered appropriate to talk about them. It's not sophisticated. Nevertheless, they're the things that really come in handy when the bottom drops out . . . and believe me, it eventually will!

So at the risk of being viewed as unsophisticated, Insight for Living Ministries has put together *Insight's Bible Reading Guide: New Testament*. This little volume will guide you through reading the New Testament this year, with helpful devotionals each week to highlight the Bible's practical importance in our lives.

God the Father, the Lord Jesus Christ, and the Holy Spirit work together to guide, inspire, and empower us . . . and we are all learners with so much more to learn. We're all people who discover the truth from His Word. And we all need the truth. What better way to get a grasp on it than by reading God's Word regularly?

May you be encouraged verse by verse.

Chuck Swindoll

Charles R. Swindoll

KEEPING TO THE WAY:
WHY WE SHOULD READ THE BIBLE

Reading the Bible daily has become one of the calling cards of being a "good Christian." Preachers and teachers regularly mark it as a sign of maturity. Believers in the pews often feel guilty when they haven't read their Bibles for a few days . . . or months. There's only one problem: *God's Word never commands us to have a private and personal Bible-reading time.*

Let that sink in a minute.

While the Bible never commands us to have a personal Bible-reading time, God's Word does make numerous commands regarding our knowledge of Scripture. Paul exhorted Timothy to "give attention to the public reading of Scripture, to exhortation and teaching" (1 Timothy 4:13). The Psalms teach us that the righteous person "meditates" on God's law "day and night" (Psalm 1:2), and the psalmist himself made a point to treasure God's Word in his heart (119:11). God clearly wanted His people to hear His Word and commit that Word to memory so they could benefit from it in daily life. But the command for individual believers to read their Bibles on their own is simply not present.

And for good reason.

For most of human history, including during the years that the Bible was being written, God's people had two significant limitations to reading the Bible: ability and access. Most people through history have been illiterate — unable to read. Further, before the printing press was invented around AD 1440, most people had no access to personal copies of the Bible. So, to encourage people to read the Bible on their own would have seemed strange and, well, impossible.

But the few people who had both the ability to read and access to Scripture have, for more than three millennia, made it a point to read it. Recognizing the fundamental importance of God's Word to the lives of God's people, these few read and faithfully shared it with those who could not read for themselves. Only in the last five hundred years or so, with the coming of Gutenberg's press and the persistence of reformers like Martin Luther, have people far and wide gained access to their own copies of God's Word.

In light of that deep and meaningful tradition, Christians today make it a point to encourage reading the Bible. But it isn't simply because of a tradition that we read. Believers throughout history have recognized the practical benefits of reading God's Word. As a result of reading Scripture, God's people grow in several ways:

1. **We Know God:** When we follow through with our commitment to reading the Bible, we come to know God more deeply. We see His character on display in His great deeds and mighty miracles. We see the beauty of His nature as He condescends to reveal Himself to His creation.

2. **We Know Ourselves:** Reading the Bible regularly increases the chances that we will see ourselves the way God sees us. Human beings have fallen and struggle in the morass of sin. But for those of us who believe, God sees us as His holy and beloved children.

3. **We Know Deliverance:** Bible reading also makes us aware of the deep, abiding, and hopeful message of Scripture— God seeks to redeem and re-create His broken creation. Through faith in His Son Jesus alone, we have hope for the future.

4. **We Know How to Live:** Finally, reading the Bible helps us understand how God wants us to live our lives, how we can keep to His way. We can know the three previous items backward and forward, but if God's Word doesn't work itself out in our lives—if that knowledge never moves from our heads to our hearts—then maybe we don't know as much as we think we do.

In the end, the truth of the matter is this: we read the Bible to know Him and be known by Him. We read to humble ourselves. We read to experience deliverance by God from sin and shame. We read to live as His faithful representatives during our time on earth.

Ultimately, we read because we love Him. And because we love Him, we love and obey His Word (Psalm 119:97, 127, 167). When we love and obey His Word, our love for God flourishes and deepens. And as our love for God grows, our passion for His Word increases, which leads again to an ever-deepening love for our Lord.

With such a beautiful cycle before us, what better reason do we need?

How to Use This Book

This book is divided into fifty-two weekly sections. Each week includes five readings, giving you time to reflect on what you've read or catch up on your reading each week if you miss a day here or there. You will also find that each reading includes passages from Psalms or Proverbs, so you'll enjoy reading those two books throughout the year.

Finally, we have included one devotional per week, designed to give you extra insight into one of the passages you'll be reading that week. Use the blank lines on each page to record a few thoughts, if you're inclined.

And most of all, enjoy your time in the New Testament. It is sure to become one of the richest times of your day.

INSIGHT'S
Bible Reading Guide
NEW TESTAMENT

All Scripture is inspired by God and profitable for teaching, for reproof, for correction, [and] for training in righteousness.
— 2 Timothy 3:16

Week 1

Monday: As Promised — God with Us
- ☐ *Matthew 1*
- ☐ *Proverbs 1:1–7*

Tuesday: From Bethlehem to Egypt to Nazareth
- ☐ *Matthew 2*
- ☐ *Proverbs 1:8–19*

Wednesday: John the Baptizer Points to Jesus
- ☐ *Matthew 3*
- ☐ *Proverbs 1:20–33*

Thursday: Jesus's Temptation and Early Ministry
- ☐ *Matthew 4*
- ☐ *Proverbs 2:1–9*

Friday: Jesus Preaches God's Standard for His Kingdom
- ☐ *Matthew 5*
- ☐ *Proverbs 2:10–22*

What I Want to Remember . . .

_____

_____

_____

_____

If there is one word I would use to describe the life of obedience, it would be the word change. *It is impossible for us to live a life of obedience if we are unwilling to change. So, let's not be afraid of new adventures. Let's welcome them.*

—*Charles R. Swindoll*

A Strategic Move

Few went to Nazareth unless they had to. The city sat off the beaten path, high on a hill. Yet it was the perfect place for the boy Jesus to grow up in seclusion, away from the grasp of any who might seek to harm Him (Matthew 2:21–23).

Years later, however, at the beginning of His ministry, Jesus moved His base of operations from Nazareth to the bustling city of Capernaum. Matthew noted that this move fulfilled "what was spoken through Isaiah the prophet" (4:14). While several cities along the shore could have fulfilled this prophecy, it seems Jesus's selection of Capernaum had more deliberate purposes.

A thriving fishing village, Capernaum straddled the international highway that stretched from Syria to Egypt. By choosing Capernaum, Jesus selected a city that enjoyed a constant flow of people who could carry His message to many places. And that's just what happened. Travelers took the news not only north into Syria (4:24) but also into "Galilee and the Decapolis and Jerusalem and Judea and from beyond the Jordan" (4:25).

In our lives and ministries, we must do more than merely exist. We need to live our lives strategically. What represents the best use of our time for God's glory? In what location or vocation can we best serve the Lord? Sometimes, these answers require a major move—as was the case with Jesus. But sometimes, we simply need to change our thinking and ask ourselves, *Is the kingdom of God really the goal of my life?*[1]

Week 2

Monday: Holy Living — Practical and Hypocritical
- ☐ Matthew 6
- ☐ Proverbs 3:1–12

Tuesday: The Narrow Gate into God's Kingdom
- ☐ Matthew 7
- ☐ Proverbs 3:13–26

Wednesday: Jesus's Healings Confirm His Message
- ☐ Matthew 8
- ☐ Proverbs 3:27–35

Thursday: The Opposition Begins
- ☐ Matthew 9
- ☐ Proverbs 4:1–9

Friday: Jesus Sends the Apostles to Preach the Kingdom
- ☐ Matthew 10
- ☐ Proverbs 4:10–19

What I Want to Remember . . .

_____

_____

_____

_____

God doesn't say, "I'll meet your greeds." He says, "I'll meet your needs." Resist the temptation to worry. Leave alone the things you cannot handle, because if you occupy yourself with them, you won't enjoy what you have.

—Charles R. Swindoll

Worry on the Mount

Multitudes thronged to Galilee to see Jesus. The Lord delivered His most famous sermon on a slope beside the northern shore of the Sea of Galilee. The traditional location on the Mount of Beatitudes provides ample space for large crowds.

In springtime, the hillside bursts with grass and flowers. Jesus drew on this setting to illustrate simple truths: "Do not be worried about your life . . . Look at the birds of the air . . . Observe how the lilies of the field grow" (Matthew 6:25–26, 28). Jesus called the people, "you of little faith" (6:30), because they sought immediate provision for tomorrow's needs instead of trusting God to provide for daily essentials as He saw fit.

The real struggle for people—both then and now—boils down to issues of control. For some reason, we feel more in control when we fret about our lives. But worry moves the burden of providing from God's shoulders to ours—a load He never intended us to bear. When we seek first God's kingdom, we yield to His control of our lives. Moreover, we come to see *all things*—even working for food and clothing—as opportunities to represent the coming of His kingdom in the world and the growth of His righteousness in our hearts.

On a gentle slope in Galilee, Jesus used simple illustrations we also can see in our land—birds, flowers, and grass. God's continual care of these things gives testimony that He will provide for us too . . . just as He always has.[2]

Week 3

Monday: Reassurance for John . . . and Rest for the Weary
- ☐ *Matthew 11*
- ☐ *Proverbs 4:20–27*

Tuesday: Pivot! Jesus Understands That Israel Will Reject Him
- ☐ *Matthew 12*
- ☐ *Proverbs 5:1–14*

Wednesday: Jesus Changes His Teaching Method
- ☐ *Matthew 13*
- ☐ *Proverbs 5:15–23*

Thursday: The Training of the Twelve Begins
- ☐ *Matthew 14*
- ☐ *Proverbs 6:1–11*

Friday: Jesus Extends His Ministry to Gentiles
- ☐ *Matthew 15*
- ☐ *Proverbs 6:12–19*

What I Want to Remember . . .

_____

_____

_____

_____

Distance from God is a frightening thing. God will never adjust His agenda to fit ours. He will not speed His pace to catch up with ours; we need to slow our pace in order to recover our walk with Him.

—Charles R. Swindoll

Letting Truth Take Root

After Jesus healed people in Capernaum, the religious leaders attributed His miracles to Satan (Matthew 12:22–29). Up to that point, Jesus's message had offered Israel the long-awaited kingdom of God, but now Jesus saw that Israel would reject His offer. So, Jesus shifted His message from preparing the nation for the kingdom to preparing the disciples for the church.

That same day, Jesus taught a large crowd from a boat. This event most likely occurred at a small cove along the north shore of the Sea of Galilee. One study revealed that about 14,000 people could fit on that hillside and still hear a lone voice from the cove below. Within this natural theater, Jesus "spoke many things to them in parables" (13:1–3)—no longer in direct discourse.

When Jesus's disciples asked why He changed His method, Jesus answered that parables served to reveal truth to those willing to receive it—and to conceal truth from those unwilling. Jesus's parable of the sower who scattered seed on various types of soil represents the various responses to God's Word—from the hard heart that ignores the truth to the soft heart that hears and applies it (13:18–23).

The story calls us each to examine our own personal response to the Bible. Do we truly listen to God's Word in order for Him to change us? Do our hearts long to bear fruit for the Lord? Or like the throng along the shore that day, do we gather just to hear stories from a gifted teacher? [3]

Week 4

Monday: Jesus Teaches the Twelve about His Death
- ☐ Matthew 16
- ☐ Proverbs 6:20–35

Tuesday: Jesus Reassures the Twelve about His Glory
- ☐ Matthew 17
- ☐ Proverbs 7:1–5

Wednesday: Stumbling Blocks and Building Blocks
- ☐ Matthew 18
- ☐ Proverbs 7:6–23

Thursday: The Spiritual Life Takes Commitment
- ☐ Matthew 19
- ☐ Proverbs 7:24–27

Friday: Greatness Is Selfless Service
- ☐ Matthew 20
- ☐ Proverbs 8:1–11

What I Want to Remember . . .

_____

_____

_____

Funny thing about the cross—in our day, it's a beautiful thing. We put it in mosaic lighting. We frame it in lovely metal. We pair it with jewels . . . on our persons, our purses, and our Bibles. People of the first century would gasp to see such things! It would be like wearing a hangman's noose on your lapel or adorning your neck with an electric chair! Make no mistake; the cross has always been a symbol of death.
—Charles R. Swindoll

TAKING THE HIGH VIEW

Jesus's preparation of the disciples for the church age included teaching that He would die in Jerusalem and rise again (Matthew 16:21). On the heels of this unthinkable statement, He made another just as fantastic: "If anyone wishes to come after Me, he must deny himself, and take up his cross and follow Me" (16:24). The cross exposed the disciples' expectations about privileged positions in the kingdom. But Jesus said discipleship also included the obligation to crucify selfish desires.

Christ didn't remove the hope of His kingdom; He simply relegated it to its proper place. Six days later, Jesus took Peter, James, and John from the region of Caesarea Philippi to a "high mountain," probably snowcapped Mount Hermon (17:1). There, Jesus's appearance changed. His face shone like the sun; His clothes became dazzling white—a sight made even more glorious by the snow.

These scenes, side by side, no doubt seemed a wild contradiction—Jesus's death and Jesus's glory. But Christ revealed these extremes so one could strengthen the other. He provided assurance of His coming kingdom to the disciples He had commanded to take up their crosses (see 1 Peter 5:1, 10).

The cross reveals our expectations. How do we respond to the harsh reality of self-sacrifice? Only the promise of heaven provides the stamina to follow a crucified Savior, putting selfish ambitions aside. We shoulder our crosses only by scaling the mountain and gazing on the glory of One who bore the cross before us . . . and for us.[4]

Week 5

Monday: Entering Jerusalem . . . and Cleaning House
- [ ] Matthew 21
- [ ] Proverbs 8:12–21

Tuesday: Trying to Trap Jesus (Are You Kidding?)
- [ ] Matthew 22
- [ ] Proverbs 8:22–36

Wednesday: Woe to the Scribes and Pharisees!
- [ ] Matthew 23
- [ ] Proverbs 9:1–12

Thursday: End-Times Lessons on the Mount of Olives
- [ ] Matthew 24
- [ ] Proverbs 9:13–18

Friday: The Kingdom Is Coming—Stay Ready
- [ ] Matthew 25
- [ ] Proverbs 10:1–10

What I Want to Remember . . .

_____

_____

_____

_____

_____

Perfection is one thing. It's Christ's domain. But authenticity is ours. And that's the least you can expect from a Christian—integrity, responsibility, purity, honesty.

—Charles R. Swindoll

JESUS WANTS FRUIT

The road Jesus walked from Jericho to Jerusalem for His final Passover passed through Bethany and Bethphage at the south-eastern slope of the Mount of Olives, just east of Jerusalem. As Jesus approached Bethphage (which means "house of unripe figs"), He directed two disciples to retrieve a donkey on which He would enter Jerusalem.

When Jesus entered the temple area, He found the Court of the Gentiles — the area for Gentiles to worship — filled with markets and moneychangers. Jesus promptly cleaned house, saying, "It is written, 'My house shall be called a house of prayer'; but you are making it a 'robbers' den'" (Matthew 21:13).

The next morning, Jesus returned to Jerusalem along the same road; this time, He noticed a fig tree in leaf, which ordinarily would have indicated fig buds. But the tree offered only leaves. Jesus cursed the tree — not in a fit of anger, but in illustration of what He had seen in the Jewish leaders and the temple: there was no fruit present, though all indications suggested otherwise.

A few days later, Jesus told His disciples He had chosen them for a particular reason: "that you would go and bear fruit, and that your fruit would remain" (John 15:16). Jesus desires the same for us.

The lives of the religious *always* bear leaves . . . but not always figs. When Jesus looks at our lives, He expects to find faith lived out authentically. He wants to find us fruitful. In fact, that's why He chose us.[5]

Week 6

Monday: The Passion of Christ Begins
- ☐ Matthew 26
- ☐ Proverbs 10:11–21

Tuesday: Mock Trials . . . an Agonizing Death . . . an Ignoble Burial
- ☐ Matthew 27
- ☐ Proverbs 10:22–32

Wednesday: He Is Risen! Now Make Disciples!
- ☐ Matthew 28
- ☐ Proverbs 11:1–11

Thursday: Jesus Preaches the Kingdom among Distractions
- ☐ Mark 1
- ☐ Proverbs 11:12–21

Friday: The Son of Man Demonstrates His Authority
- ☐ Mark 2
- ☐ Proverbs 11:22–31

What I Want to Remember . . .

_____

_____

_____

For every disciple there is a purpose to be fulfilled. It's different for different disciples. Only One went to the cross. You don't need to go to a literal cross, to be nailed there to die. That has already been done—once for all. Let me put it this way: for every disciple there is a mission, a particular mandate, a heaven-sent assignment. Please remember, it's not something you choose; it's something God chooses.

—*Charles R. Swindoll*

GARDEN PLACES

At the base of the Mount of Olives today lies a small grotto that produced evidence of an ancient "oil press," the meaning of the name *Gethsemane*. Byzantine Christians believed that Jesus left His disciples at this place while He went a stone's throw away to pray in the garden. "Sit here," Jesus told them, "while I go over there and pray" (Matthew 26:36). Then, taking Peter, James, and John with Him into the garden, Jesus said to them, "Remain here and keep watch with Me" (26:38). Going a bit farther, Jesus fell prostrate and prayed with passion.

Today, the Church of All Nations covers the traditional place where Jesus prayed and displays a beautiful mosaic of the event. Ancient olive trees stand in the garden, but it's unlikely they ever beheld Christ in prayer, as the Romans cut down all trees in the region during the siege on Jerusalem in AD 70.

Still, entering the garden of Gethsemane, one can imagine the scenes and almost retrace Jesus's steps along the places Matthew mentioned: the grotto, the garden, the place of prayer. And a stunning insight occurs when one turns around and sees the walls of Jerusalem so close behind: Jesus could have easily seen the soldiers coming to arrest Him! In fact, He said, "Here comes my betrayer!" (26:46 NIV). Jesus could see those who would lead Him to death; still He chose to stay in the garden out of obedience to the Father . . . and out of love for us.[6]

Week 7

Monday: Choosing an Inner Circle
- ☐ Mark 3
- ☐ Proverbs 12:1–10

Tuesday: Three Parables and a Miracle
- ☐ Mark 4
- ☐ Proverbs 12:11–19

Wednesday: Jesus Heals the Demon-Possessed and the Sick
- ☐ Mark 5
- ☐ Proverbs 12:20–28

Thursday: A Holy Man and a Hostile Woman
- ☐ Mark 6
- ☐ Proverbs 13:1–12

Friday: From Jerusalem to Tyre
- ☐ Mark 7
- ☐ Proverbs 13:13–25

What I Want to Remember . . .

_____

_____

_____

_____

What insight! What determination! What faith! Can you even imagine the relief that dear mother and daughter felt? For the first time, they could sleep through the night. For the first time, she wasn't afraid to leave her daughter alone. For the first time, mother and daughter could embrace and weep, overjoyed because of Jesus's deliverance.

—Charles R. Swindoll

Determination Pays Off

According to the Pharisees of Jesus's day, God's favor rested on people based on their actions and their physical heritage. Early in Mark 7, Jesus addressed the first of these misguided ideals, making clear that the Pharisees' code was man-made and not honoring to God (Mark 7:9, 13).

To address the second misconception, Jesus turned north and left Israel (7:24–30; see also Matthew 15:21–28). As Jesus moved into the region of Tyre and Sidon, His reputation preceded Him. Not long after His arrival, a woman with a demon-possessed daughter sought out Jesus for help. The only problem? She was a Gentile.

Jesus met her initial plea for help with an abrupt response: His mission was to the Israelites first. It wasn't proper for Him to "take the children's bread and throw it to the dogs" (Mark 7:27). Embracing her lowly position—one that Jesus had recognized—the Gentile woman persisted, asking for "crumbs" from the Master's table, to which Jesus responded by healing the woman's daughter then and there (7:28–29).

In healing this woman's daughter, Jesus made two things abundantly clear. First, God's offer of salvation is available to anyone, no matter who one's parents are. Second, persistence in one's faith yields a glorious result. The glory may come only after a lifetime of struggle, but Jesus showed us that it will indeed come to those who believe.

Week 8

Monday: Cross Talk: Opening the Eyes of Squinting Disciples
- ☐ Mark 8
- ☐ Proverbs 14:1–11

Tuesday: Transfiguration Reassures That a Kingdom Is Coming
- ☐ Mark 9
- ☐ Proverbs 14:12–22

Wednesday: What It Means to Be Great
- ☐ Mark 10
- ☐ Proverbs 14:23–35

Thursday: Entering Jerusalem to Cheers and Jeers
- ☐ Mark 11
- ☐ Proverbs 15:1–11

Friday: Final Teachings in the Temple
- ☐ Mark 12
- ☐ Proverbs 15:12–22

What I Want to Remember . . .

_____

_____

_____

_____

When we come to Christ, our spiritual blindness is removed; the scales are taken away; we're given sight. And we expect our sight to be perfect, but it isn't. I have discovered that the process of cultivating good spiritual vision is a lifetime task.

—Charles R. Swindoll

Sight and Insight

"Having eyes, do you not see?" (Mark 8:18).

Jesus's question to His disciples revealed the purpose for the miracle that followed. When Jesus gave sight in stages to the blind man in Bethsaida, the miracle represented the gradual insight He was giving to the disciples.

Jesus began opening His men's eyes when He took them north to Caesarea Philippi. There, in an area surrounded by idols, Jesus asked His disciples what the people thought of Him and also how *they* viewed Him. Peter's response, "You are the Christ" (8:29), revealed that he understood *who* Jesus was, but Peter's next response revealed that neither he nor the rest of the apostles understood *for what purpose* Jesus had come.

When Jesus revealed for the first time that He would die, Peter responded by rebuking the Son of God! Can you imagine? Although Peter and the other disciples had a correct view of Christ, they saw Him through the fog of their own expectations. It would take the cross to open their eyes.

Just as the blind man saw in stages and the disciples understood in stages, so we have much to learn about the Lord we worship. A God who is infinite reveals Himself to the finite bit by bit. For starters, Christ did not come to fulfill our interests and goals but that we should follow His.

It often takes a lifetime to open our eyes to that reality.[7]

Week 9

Monday: A Hint of Things to Come
- ☐ Mark 13
- ☐ Proverbs 15:23–33

Tuesday: Jesus's Final Moments with His Friends
- ☐ Mark 14
- ☐ Proverbs 16:1–11

Wednesday: History's Darkest Day
- ☐ Mark 15
- ☐ Proverbs 16:12–22

Thursday: History's Brightest Day
- ☐ Mark 16
- ☐ Proverbs 16:23–33

Friday: Angelic Visits and Miracle Babies
- ☐ Luke 1
- ☐ Proverbs 17:1–14

What I Want to Remember . . .

_____

_____

_____

To be like Jesus—that is our goal, plain and simple. It sounds like a peaceful, relaxing, easy objective. But stop and think. Jesus learned obedience through suffering. So do we. He endured all kinds of temptations. So must we. To be like Jesus is neither easy nor quick nor natural. It's impossible in the flesh, slow in coming, supernatural in scope. Only Jesus can accomplish it within us.

—Charles R. Swindoll

People-Stress

There's no stress like people-stress. Endless task lists can't compete with the tension of relationships out of sync. Read Mark 14 through that fractured lens, and you'll be amazed by the incredible people-stress Jesus endured.

First, the high priests and scholars put a hit out on Him (Mark 14:1).

Then, at a dinner in Bethany, Jesus stood between a party-crasher who wanted to bless Him and others who were incensed by her (14:3–5). One of those irate guests was Judas, Jesus's own disciple, who stormed from the party, hellbent on betraying Him (14:10).

A couple of days later, when Jesus told His men they would fall away after He died, they didn't believe Him (14:29–31).

Later, Jesus Himself wrestled as He talked with His Father about the next day's events (14:36). At Jesus's most vulnerable hour, when all He had asked was for them to pray for Him, His closest friends fell asleep (14:37).

Afterward, soldiers marched Jesus off in chains . . . alone. He endured the bogus trials through the night . . . alone. The next morning, He went to the cross . . . alone.

Jesus understands the stress of being misunderstood . . . betrayed by friends . . . rejected by loved ones . . . and mistreated by the system.

Not only does He understand the people-stress you face today . . . He's lived it.

Week 10

Monday: Birth and Early Years of the Son of Man
- ☐ Luke 2
- ☐ Proverbs 17:15–28

Tuesday: John Prepares the Way and Baptizes the Lord
- ☐ Luke 3
- ☐ Proverbs 18:1–12

Wednesday: Jesus's Temptation and Early Galilee Ministry
- ☐ Luke 4
- ☐ Proverbs 18:13–24

Thursday: The First Disciples See Miraculous Healings
- ☐ Luke 5
- ☐ Proverbs 19:1–10

Friday: The Twelve Apostles Hear the Sermon on the Plain
- ☐ Luke 6
- ☐ Proverbs 19:11–20

What I Want to Remember . . .

_____

_____

_____

_____

_____

*The true repentant sinner is seized with the enormity of his or her sin
and refuses to excuse it. He or she blames no one else but addresses the
sin and comes to terms with it, with the help of the living God.*

—Charles R. Swindoll

SMOOTHING THE ROUGH EDGES

The gospel of Luke indicates that John the Baptist specifically fulfilled Isaiah's prophecy of a voice crying in the wilderness to prepare the way for the Messiah (Isaiah 40:3). The wilderness of Judea today sits virtually unchanged since the time of John. Deep valleys, high hills, and rough, rocky paths set apart this barren wasteland where John preached, "Make ready the way of the Lord, make His paths straight" (Luke 3:4).

In ancient times, when a king visited a foreign land, he often sent workers ahead to smooth out the roads so he could travel unimpeded. In preparing the way for the King of Kings, John the Baptist pointed to the rough terrain around him and compared it to the hard hearts he saw in the people. John used the physical geography in his message to communicate the need for spiritual change in their hearts: "Every ravine will be filled, and every mountain and hill will be brought low; the crooked will become straight, and the rough roads smooth" (3:5). The simple command that characterized John's message—"repent"—referred to a change of mind that should produce a change of action.

What geographic illustration would John use to describe your heart today: rocky crags or level pathways? What in your life would Christ have to walk around if He came to you right now? Any weak ravines need filling . . . or proud peaks need leveling?

The Lord is committed to making these rough places a smooth path on which He can walk unhindered.[8]

Week 11

Monday: Is Christ the One? His Works Prove It!
- ☐ *Luke 7*
- ☐ *Proverbs 19:21–29*

Tuesday: For Whom Did He Come? *Any* Who Would Hear and Believe
- ☐ *Luke 8*
- ☐ *Proverbs 20:1–10*

Wednesday: The Power and Glory of Christ and the Cost of Following Him
- ☐ *Luke 9*
- ☐ *Proverbs 20:11–20*

Thursday: The Privilege of Following Christ
- ☐ *Luke 10*
- ☐ *Proverbs 20:21–30*

Friday: A Gathering Storm of Opposition
- ☐ *Luke 11*
- ☐ *Proverbs 21:1–10*

What I Want to Remember . . .

_____

_____

_____

_____

The gentle wind of compromise is a lot more devastating than the sudden jolt of misfortune. That's why walking on a wire is harder than standing up in a storm.

—*Charles R. Swindoll*

To All Who Will Listen

In wrapping up His explanation of the parable of the soils, Jesus mentioned repeatedly the importance of listening. Those who listen well develop a strong faith they can share (Luke 8:15), receive more illumination and insight into the ways of God (8:18), and are counted as God's family (8:21).

The act of listening is crucial.

But many of us share a common trouble with listening: we try to make new information jibe with our established preconceptions. Too often we don't evaluate those preconceptions and allow them to be challenged by the new message we've heard. Two brief encounters at the end of Luke 9 make this truth plain.

In the first, a man blurted out that he would follow Jesus anywhere. The Master's reply revealed the man's preconception: following Jesus would surely bring him into a comfortable living. Jesus, however, pointed out that even if the man were to follow, he would have no guarantee even of a roof over his head (9:57–58). In the second, another man saw the call of Jesus as a casual invitation that took second place to receiving his earthly inheritance (9:59–60).

In both encounters, Jesus had to correct the men's preconceptions before they could listen clearly. Following Jesus carries no promise of earthly security, and obedience leaves no room for being double-minded.

Learn to listen well by asking God to challenge your preconceptions. Use the pure teachings of the Scripture to reset your priorities and then follow God's Word in obedience.

Week 12

Monday: Daily Life Lessons
- [ ] *Luke 12*
- [ ] *Proverbs 21:11–20*

Tuesday: Following Jesus Around
- [ ] *Luke 13*
- [ ] *Proverbs 21:21–31*

Wednesday: Defining Discipleship
- [ ] *Luke 14*
- [ ] *Proverbs 22:1–10*

Thursday: Seeking the Lost
- [ ] *Luke 15*
- [ ] *Proverbs 22:11–21*

Friday: Of Money, Marriage, and Mercy
- [ ] *Luke 16*
- [ ] *Proverbs 22:22–29*

What I Want to Remember . . .

_____

_____

_____

_____

In Luke's gospel, we see Jesus as a man. He touches the hurting. He embraces the broken and the bruised. He seeks and saves the lost. Nowhere else do we see stories quite like these, stories that emphasize the compassion of the Savior, of the man Jesus Christ.

—Charles R. Swindoll

Lost and Found

If you've ever lost your credit card, you know the panic that sets in after you've checked your pockets and your wallet, between the car seats and couch cushions . . . only to come up empty-handed.

That panic intensifies if, instead of your credit card, you've lost your dog. Someone left the back gate open and now that lovable family member is missing.

But nothing can compare with losing a child — the one with your eyes and his or her own will. If that child left by choice, it pains you more. How many nights do you leave the porch light on?

In Luke 15, when Jesus told the three stories of something lost, He touched a nerve. Everyone is missing something — including God the Father. Jesus knew that all who heard or would hear these stories would be, at some point in their lives, far from God — on the run, chasing their own rebellion.

Perhaps Jesus thought the best way to picture His Father's heart for the lost was to show His search-and-rescue operation. So Jesus pictured Him as being like the woman who tore up her house looking for a lost coin, or the shepherd who walked the hills calling for His lost animal, or the father who kicked up dirt in a full-on sprint to embrace his returning prodigal child.

That's the picture Jesus wanted to paint of His Father's love . . . just in case anyone in the crowd was far from home.

Week 13

Monday: Forgive — Even Seven Times a Day
- ☐ Luke 17
- ☐ Proverbs 23:1–9

Tuesday: Pray and Do Not Lose Heart
- ☐ Luke 18
- ☐ Proverbs 23:10–21

Wednesday: Blessed Is the King Who Comes
- ☐ Luke 19
- ☐ Proverbs 23:22–35

Thursday: By What Authority?
- ☐ Luke 20
- ☐ Proverbs 24:1–12

Friday: Be Alert and Always Pray
- ☐ Luke 21
- ☐ Proverbs 24:13–22

What I Want to Remember . . .

_____

_____

_____

We often find ourselves bogged down in our spiritual growth because the challenges before us look absolutely impossible. Do you realize that whatever you're calling an "impossibility" is something God says is "nothing" to Him? Nothing. Think about that which seems most impossible. Now think about this: nothing is impossible with God. Will you ask the Lord to handle your specific impossibility, and then leave it with Him in a faith that simply will not doubt?

—Charles R. Swindoll

IMPOSSIBILITIES — GOD'S SPECIALTY

We know the story well. Pharaoh's hard-charging army on one side, the Red Sea on the other, and the Hebrews sandwiched in between. It was an impossible situation without a human solution. Moses said, "Do not fear! Stand by and see the salvation of the LORD which He will accomplish for you today" (Exodus 14:13). The Lord acted and saw the sons of Israel safely through the parted sea; then He drowned the Egyptian army as they tried to follow.

Somehow, when we face impossible situations, we lose sight of God's Word. We forget that He says *nothing* is impossible for Him (Luke 18:27). Instead, we look to our own plans and resources. We find it difficult to apply the Bible to our impossibility. We don't see any way out. We feel trapped. We forget to pray and trust in the Lord. Often, we act on our own rather than wait on God, and the situation becomes even worse. Like the Hebrews fleeing the Egyptian army, we feel sandwiched, unable to wiggle our way out.

Are you struggling to see hope in your difficult circumstances? It's at these moments that God does His very best work.

We all face remarkable opportunities brilliantly disguised as impossible situations. And God specializes in impossible situations. If we turn to Him and trust Him, He *will* follow through. Do it today!

Week 14

Monday: A Supper, an Arrest, and a Trial
- ☐ Luke 22
- ☐ Proverbs 24:23–34

Tuesday: The Death of the King
- ☐ Luke 23
- ☐ Proverbs 25:1–10

Wednesday: Life after the Grave
- ☐ Luke 24
- ☐ Proverbs 25:11–20

Thursday: Behold the Lamb of God
- ☐ John 1
- ☐ Proverbs 25:21–28

Friday: Vintage Jesus
- ☐ John 2
- ☐ Proverbs 26:1–14

What I Want to Remember . . .

_____

_____

_____

_____

If Jesus had not risen from the dead, we would have no message. We would have nothing to share. We would be no better off than people proclaiming man's religion — started by humans and sustained by humans. The Christian message without the resurrection is just one more message about a good man who lived and died for a good cause.
—*Charles R. Swindoll*

TOUCH ME AND SEE

When Jesus was born, God the Son — or "the Word" as John called Him — took on human flesh (John 1:14). For many, the incarnation of Jesus relates to His sympathy with our weakness (Hebrews 4:15) or His provision of salvation (Philippians 2:8–11). However, Jesus's physical body has implications not just before the cross but also after.

After His resurrection, Jesus appeared bodily to many, among them a group of His followers in Jerusalem (Luke 24:36–49). Mere days after His resurrection, Jesus appeared in their midst and the people were startled, believing they were seeing a ghost. However, Jesus took pains to show them that He was truly there — not in some disembodied fashion but in His actual, physical body. He was, in fact, bodily present.

Jesus first offered as proof His hands and feet, no doubt a reference to the wounds the Lord suffered on the cross. He encouraged them, "Touch Me and see," and He even ate a piece of broiled fish to make clear His physical presence (24:39).

Jesus's bodily resurrection is crucially important for the Christian faith because it confirms that He truly did conquer the grave. Since Jesus overcame death, we who follow the crucified Savior will also overcome death. Just as He was raised from the dead, so too will we be raised from the dead, overcoming the grave and living with Him bodily and spiritually for eternity (Romans 6:3–8). The promise of this glorious life gives hope to Christians everywhere.

Week 15

Monday: Meeting by Moonlight
- [ ] John 3
- [ ] Proverbs 26:15–28

Tuesday: Meeting by Noonday Sun
- [ ] John 4
- [ ] Proverbs 27:1–13

Wednesday: Meeting at the Healing Pool
- [ ] John 5
- [ ] Proverbs 27:14–27

Thursday: Meeting by the Shore
- [ ] John 6
- [ ] Proverbs 28:1–14

Friday: Meeting at the Temple
- [ ] John 7
- [ ] Proverbs 28:15–28

What I Want to Remember . . .

_____

_____

_____

_____

Have you ever studied Jesus's approach to talking with people? He didn't always fill the space with answers for them. Let's learn to do that with our fellow learners. Let's give them room to think and answer for themselves.

—Charles R. Swindoll

ONE-ON-ONE CONVERSATIONS

If *Candid Camera* had existed in biblical times, we could have witnessed some interesting reactions from those who met with Jesus! Shock and surprise followed Him, especially in the vignettes captured in John 3–5.

First, there's Jesus and local teacher Nicodemus (John 3). Hesitant for the world to know he was intrigued with the Rabbi, Nicodemus requested they meet at night. Imagine the question mark that must've screwed on his face when Nicodemus asked about salvation and Jesus coined the phrase, "You must be born again" (3:5).

Then there's Jesus at the well in chapter 4, talking to a woman everyone else ignored. Imagine her shock when He asked for a drink . . . and then told her the most intimate details of her personal life.

We see Him next at the home of a royal official and then by the Pool of Bethesda, where we learn: when you or someone you love is sick, you'll do anything. Such was the case with the lame beggar by the pool (5:1–15) and with the royal official whose son lay dying (4:46–54). With just a word from Jesus, both witnessed miracles. Imagine their faces when they realized the healings were *for real*.

Each of these encounters with Jesus came down to one question, *Who do you say that I am?* This is the question for us too. Will you answer like Peter, declaring in faith, "You are the Christ, the Son of the living God" (Matthew 16:16)?

Week 16

Monday: The Son of God Identifies Himself
- ☐ John 8
- ☐ Proverbs 29:1–9

Tuesday: The Many Faces of Blindness
- ☐ John 9
- ☐ Proverbs 29:10–18

Wednesday: Jesus, the Good Shepherd, Is God
- ☐ John 10
- ☐ Proverbs 29:19–27

Thursday: Making a Dead Man Hear
- ☐ John 11
- ☐ Proverbs 30:1–10

Friday: An Amazing Lack of Faith
- ☐ John 12
- ☐ Proverbs 30:11–23

What I Want to Remember . . .

_____

_____

_____

_____

When you're open to God's leading and you've got His Word in your heart, a magnet will start pulling on you. You will sense a direction. It may not come quickly, but ultimately, it will come. Understand this: God doesn't operate on a 24-hour or 60-second clock. His timing is eternal.
—Charles R. Swindoll

WHEN JESUS SHOWS UP LATE

Mary and Martha of Bethany sent a message to Jesus that their brother, Lazarus, lay sick. The journey to their home would take Jesus two days of hard, hot, uphill travel. But instead of setting out immediately, Jesus stayed right where He was. When He finally did arrive, Lazarus had been dead four days. In other words, Jesus took His sweet time showing up.

From all appearances, Jesus's delay suggested a lack of ability or concern (John 11:21, 32, 37). But remarkably, Jesus delayed *because* He loved Mary, Martha . . . and Lazarus (11:5–6).

It's hard to feel God's love when we cry out to Him and He seems to ignore us. Our pain blurs what Jesus sees clearly. Jesus saw what Lazarus's death would produce—an opportunity to believe for those who would witness a miracle. He knew the sisters would grow to understand that God loved them on a level that went deeper than simply removing their pain. This is precisely how we must grow as well.

Because Jesus waited, we can know He wants to give us something more valuable than relief. Because Jesus wept (11:35), we can understand that He feels our pain and strengthens us with His presence along the path His sovereign will determines best for us. Jesus loves us enough to let us hurt so that we will gain what we could not otherwise. The Lord waits with us—and weeps—along the painful road that leads first to death . . . but then to resurrection.[9]

Week 17

Monday: Clean Feet and an Unclean Heart
- [ ] John 13
- [ ] Proverbs 30:24–33

Tuesday: A Helper Is On the Way
- [ ] John 14
- [ ] Proverbs 31:1–9

Wednesday: Vine and Vine-Dresser
- [ ] John 15
- [ ] Proverbs 31:10–20

Thursday: Predictions and Promises
- [ ] John 16
- [ ] Proverbs 31:21–31

Friday: Prayers for the Disciples and Believers
- [ ] John 17
- [ ] Psalm 1

What I Want to Remember . . .

_____

_____

_____

_____

When Jesus prayed in John 17, He was surrounded by eleven men who loved Him desperately but who were terribly disillusioned. They had been given the most profound truths they had ever heard. So what did Jesus do? He prayed for His disciples and for those who would believe His message—namely, you and me.

—*Charles R. Swindoll*

IN THIS WORLD

Just before entering the garden of Gethsemane, where Judas would betray Him, Jesus taught and prayed for His disciples. Faced with the prospect of leaving them behind, Jesus asked the Father that Jesus's disciples (and those who would eventually believe) would hold up under the pressures of life in this world.

As Jesus anticipated the difficult road for those who follow Him, He did not pray that His followers be removed from the world, but that we might avoid evil as we live within this world (John 17:15–16).

Jesus's prayer raises a question pertinent for many of His people today: Are we isolated from the world or engaged with it? In the interest of safety or convenience, have we grown disconnected from our communities and from those in need?

The prayer of Jesus encourages believers to embrace the challenges posed by living life with other people. Even though we dwell in the midst of weakness and wickedness, Jesus prayed that we be protected from evil. Our task is not to build fortresses in our lives that keep the world out but rather to live well in our neighborhoods and cities, meeting the needs of people materially and spiritually.

Consider what it means to *be in the world, not of the world*. Ponder the ways in which you might more fully embrace the spirit of Jesus's prayer, a prayer offered just as He was preparing to make the ultimate sacrifice for people everywhere.

Week 18

Monday: Trials and Denials
- ☐ *John 18*
- ☐ *Psalm 2*

Tuesday: The Son of God Dies . . . and Is Buried
- ☐ *John 19*
- ☐ *Psalm 3*

Wednesday: The Son of God Rises . . . and Appears to Mary
- ☐ *John 20*
- ☐ *Psalm 4*

Thursday: Starting Over: Follow Me
- ☐ *John 21*
- ☐ *Psalm 5*

Friday: The Son of God Commissions His Church . . . and Ascends
- ☐ *Acts 1*
- ☐ *Psalm 6*

What I Want to Remember . . .

_____

_____

_____

Sometimes, doubts force us to pursue the truth — a quest more rewarding than just being gullible and believing whatever we're told. Doubt can be the fuel that gives us energy to pursue something we have questioned for a long time . . . and find true faith. A doubter is no more a heretic than a questioner is a fool.

—Charles R. Swindoll

BELIEVING IS SEEING

Nineteenth-century archaeologist William Ramsay began his career with the assumption that the book of Acts contained careless, geographical errors written by someone ignorant of Asia Minor. However, after Ramsay traveled throughout Asia Minor (modern-day Turkey), he altered his position. He found the geography presented in Acts accurate in every detail—and he believed in Christ.

Many people demand evidence for truth they never intend to accept. Their problem isn't a lack of truth, but a suppression of it (see Romans 1:18–20). While God has no problem proving Himself, He knows that proof only goes so far. For when proof removes people's excuses, they must then respond with belief.

"Unless I see," said Thomas, ". . . I will not believe" (John 20:25). Thomas wasn't the only skeptic in the bunch. Many, if not most, of Jesus's disciples struggled with uncertainty—even after the resurrection. Jesus did all He could to affirm their faith and dispel their doubts (Matthew 28:17–20; Luke 24:38–39; Acts 1:3). But the believing part He left up to them.

It's the same with us. While proof may help our faith along, it never believes for us. Whether we face doubts about the geography of Acts, the provision for our groceries, or even the salvation of our souls, our responsibility remains the same: we must respond to the truth God has revealed by believing it.[10]

Week 19

Monday: The Birth of the Church
- ☐ Acts 2
- ☐ Psalm 7

Tuesday: Peter and John around Town
- ☐ Acts 3
- ☐ Psalm 8

Wednesday: Peter and John Defend the Gospel
- ☐ Acts 4
- ☐ Psalm 9

Thursday: The Church Grows Up
- ☐ Acts 5
- ☐ Psalm 10

Friday: Responsibilities Distributed
- ☐ Acts 6
- ☐ Psalm 11

What I Want to Remember . . .

_____

_____

_____

_____

The depth of a church is determined by the quality of its worship and instruction. The breadth of a church is determined by its commitment to fellowship and evangelism. We must keep reaching out to people who are in need. After all, that is what love is all about.

—Charles R. Swindoll

For the Sake of Unity

Being devoted to each other and to God's Word like the young church in Acts 2:42 means each of us works hard at unity in the body of Christ. The strength behind this pledge is in the sacrifice of yourself.

For the sake of unity, you give up your opinions, your entitlements, your injured feelings. Always caring, always working it out, always helping—that is how far you must go to "do life" with your brothers and sisters in Christ. You do it always because you want to honor God, not because you always like each of them. You may say, "But his opinion is wrong!" Perhaps. But if it's not in conflict with what the Bible clearly teaches, swallow your argument and agree to disagree. What clearer evidence could there be that God is at work in you?

And what if after years of patience and love, that someone still disappoints you? In frustration you may wonder, "How long do I have to put up with him?" The answer is, "Always." God is watching how we treat each other and honors every time we roll up our sleeves to do the hard thing. Though it's easier to tap dance out of relationships as soon as weaknesses begin to show, working for unity means followers of Christ love each other *in spite of each other*.

Why? Because our eyes are on the One who loves us even though we disappoint Him, the One who humbled Himself and became obedient unto death for the sake of a greater glory.

Week 20

Monday: Stephen—The First Christian Martyr
- ☐ *Acts 7*
- ☐ *Psalm 12*

Tuesday: Persecution Spreads the Gospel Flame
- ☐ *Acts 8*
- ☐ *Psalm 13*

Wednesday: Persecutor Becomes Evangelist
- ☐ *Acts 9*
- ☐ *Psalm 14*

Thursday: The Gospel Crosses the Gentile Barrier
- ☐ *Acts 10*
- ☐ *Psalm 15*

Friday: The Circle Widens as the Church Spreads to Antioch
- ☐ *Acts 11*
- ☐ *Psalm 16*

What I Want to Remember . . .

_____

_____

_____

_____

*There are various ways to describe it—turning the other cheek . . .
doing good to those who hate us . . . loving our enemies—but the action
amounts to the same thing. By doing the unexpected, we accomplish a
twofold objective: we put an end to bitterness, and we prove that love
conquers all.*

—Charles R. Swindoll

Persecution's Ironic Twist

The more the church is persecuted, the more it grows.

This has been true since the beginning when Stephen's death sparked a firestorm of persecution. The lead tormentor was Saul, who "began ravaging the church" (Acts 8:3). But ironically, the fire that was meant to consume the gospel only spread its flame. As the believers scattered, they "preached the word wherever they went" (8:4 NIV). Saul's attempt to destroy Christianity ignited an even greater movement! And to give the irony a further twist, Christ chose the ravager himself, Paul, to expand the church to the Gentile world.

Why does persecution spawn growth? Because people are drawn to the love of Christ, which flourishes under persecution's heat. Stephen prayed for his assailants just as Christ prayed for His executioners: "Lord, do not hold this sin against them!" (7:60; see also Luke 23:34). Only the Spirit of Christ in Stephen could muster such a response.

This love so divine touches a soft spot in every human heart. Our minds can't comprehend it, but our hearts long to embrace it. And so the love of Christ draws people in, and the church grows.

Is an enemy clutching stones to throw at you? View this attack not as a means of destruction but as an opportunity for Christ to shine. Respond to hatred not in kind but with Jesus's love — just as His followers have been doing since the beginning.

Week 21

Monday: Peter Escapes from Prison
- ☐ Acts 12
- ☐ Psalm 17

Tuesday: Paul's First Missionary Journey
- ☐ Acts 13
- ☐ Psalm 18:1–19

Wednesday: Paul and Barnabas Preach
- ☐ Acts 14
- ☐ Psalm 18:20–36

Thursday: Paul's Second Missionary Journey
- ☐ Acts 15
- ☐ Psalm 18:37–50

Friday: Paul and Silas in the Jail
- ☐ Acts 16
- ☐ Psalm 19

What I Want to Remember . . .

_____

_____

_____

_____

Just because you're going through turmoil, difficulty, persecution, or hardship does not necessarily mean you're out of God's will. It could mean you're right in the nucleus of it. Don't forget that.

—Charles R. Swindoll

PRAISE FROM A PRISON CELL

Tight chains. Dark cells. Hymns of praise.

If you were locked in a first-century prison cell, no doubt you'd feel the heavy chains cutting deep into your wrists and the pitch-black darkness closing in all around you. But the question is: *Would you sing hymns of praise?*

Paul and Silas did.

In Acts 16, they freed a slave girl of a demon that had enabled her to tell the future. With her masters' means of wealth gone, anger ensued, then a mob, then imprisonment for the two followers of Christ (Acts 16:16–24). We read their reaction in verse 25: "But about midnight Paul and Silas were praying and singing hymns of praise to God, and the prisoners were listening to them."

Suddenly an earthquake shook the foundation of the prison. There was their opportunity to walk right out (16:26)! But God had another purpose—they were to save the life of the Philippian jailer. Not only that, but the jailer and "his entire household rejoiced because they all believed in God" (16:34 NLT).

What was true of Paul and Silas so long ago is true of believers today: the world is watching to see how we'll respond to difficult circumstances. No matter how painful the chains or how dark our prison cells, we can have hope knowing God has a purpose for our suffering.

Like Paul and Silas, we can choose to praise God in the grimmest circumstances and shine His light into a dark world.

Week 22

Monday: Paul . . . On the Road Again
- ☐ *Acts 17*
- ☐ *Psalm 20*

Tuesday: Tent-makers Make Good Missionaries
- ☐ *Acts 18*
- ☐ *Psalm 21*

Wednesday: Miracles upon Miracles
- ☐ *Acts 19*
- ☐ *Psalm 22*

Thursday: Bound and Determined to Keep Going
- ☐ *Acts 20*
- ☐ *Psalm 23*

Friday: Doing the Right Thing . . . Not the Easy Thing
- ☐ *Acts 21*
- ☐ *Psalm 24*

What I Want to Remember . . .

_____

_____

_____

_____

If you left it unsaid, would it make any difference? If it wouldn't, why fill the air with words? I can't remember very many times I've felt sorry for things I did not say, but there have been many times I could cut out my tongue for things I have said.

—Charles R. Swindoll

He Who Argues Loudest and Longest . . .

Engaging non-Christians about matters concerning spirituality can easily become a one-sided affair, where those who impart the loudest and longest arguments become the winners—at least in their own minds.

Acts 19 records just such a one-sided debate. The pagan merchants of Ephesus were in an uproar because Paul had been teaching that "gods made with hands are no gods at all" (Acts 19:26). Paul's culturally inflammatory remarks were causing the idol-makers and the the idol-sellers to suffer financially. Apparently, the citizens of the city had been paying attention to Paul's teachings and subsequently had stopped buying these silver statues that honored the goddess Artemis.

So a maddened crowd of merchants and townspeople demanded that one of Paul's cohorts, Alexander, provide a defense for Paul's teaching. But rather than listening civilly to Alexander's argument, the Ephesians "shouted for about two hours, 'Great is Artemis of the Ephesians'" (19:34). Alexander couldn't get a word in edgewise . . . and he didn't even try to rebuff them.

Smart move.

When someone attacks your faith in Christ, try being quiet—as Alexander was—while your opponent shouts himself or herself into eventual silence. Shouting back only wears you out and certainly doesn't advance your cause. Allow the Holy Spirit to work as your guide in what to say or *not* say. Wait . . . respond only if you need to, and do so with patience and love. Eventually, you just may win a hearing.

Week 23

Monday: Life's New Direction
- ☐ Acts 22
- ☐ Psalm 25

Tuesday: Paul's Day in Court
- ☐ Acts 23
- ☐ Psalm 26

Wednesday: An Audience with the Governor
- ☐ Acts 24
- ☐ Psalm 27

Thursday: A Convincing Argument for Christ
- ☐ Acts 25
- ☐ Psalm 28

Friday: The Sad Scenario of "Almost Persuaded"
- ☐ Acts 26
- ☐ Psalm 29

What I Want to Remember . . .

_____

_____

_____

_____

_____

You are not responsible for how people respond to the truth of the gospel. Your responsibility is to give the truth. It's God's responsibility to lead them to believe it.

—Charles R. Swindoll

LIVE LIKE YOU MEAN IT

Our lives shape other people's opinions about Christ. It's true whether we know it or not; it happens whether we want it to or not. People watch us navigate our lives—especially when we meet rough waters. They watch us respond. And then they decide.

Well aware of this observant audience, Paul saw it as an opportunity to demonstrate the superiority of a life lived in Christ. During Paul's most difficult days—when he was arrested, mistreated, misunderstood, and deserted—he powerfully delivered the message of Christ.

In Caesarea, Paul captured the eyes and ears of officials, guards, and fellow prisoners. The same man who had threatened to bring Christians to their knees (Acts 7–8) then stood before a Roman governor confessing that the One he had persecuted was in fact the Son of God (23:35–26:32). The transformation that had begun on a road far from this seaside auditorium had sent Paul down a new road—one toward heaven. He spent the rest of his life persuading others to join him, fearlessly testifying before crowds and to everyone he met.

His public influence was undeniable. However, some of his best witnessing happened during the lonely hours he spent in prison, trusting God in the dark. How many have read the words he wrote alone during those days and, by his testimony, stepped onto the heaven-bound road?

Wherever you are, live faithfully. Someone who needs Jesus will be watching.

Week 24

Monday: Island Shipwreck on the Voyage to Caesar
- ☐ Acts 27
- ☐ Psalm 30

Tuesday: Healing in Malta, Preaching in Rome
- ☐ Acts 28
- ☐ Psalm 31

Wednesday: God's Righteousness Revealed to a Sinful World
- ☐ Romans 1
- ☐ Psalm 32

Thursday: The Righteous and the Self-Righteous
- ☐ Romans 2
- ☐ Psalm 33

Friday: Sin, Satisfaction, and Salvation
- ☐ Romans 3
- ☐ Psalm 34

What I Want to Remember . . .

_____

_____

_____

_____

God sees us wallowing around in the swamp of our sin. He also sees us looking to Jesus Christ and trusting Him completely by faith to cleanse us. And therefore, though we come to God in all of our darkness, He says to us, "Declared righteous! Forgiven! Pardoned!" That's what justification is.
— *Charles R. Swindoll*

48

Deliverance by Decree

The piercing light of the gospel can seem dim until we comprehend three things: our true sinful condition, our Savior's mission, and how we, ruined sinners, are saved. Romans 3:9–30 is the centerpiece of gospel clarity.

Like corpses, all people are spiritually lifeless on their own. Check the numbers. How many are sinful? "All" (Romans 3:9, 12, 19, 23). How many understand, do right, seek and follow God? "None," as in "*not even one*" (3:10–12). The sinful condition of humankind is *universal ruin* (3:9–20).

Is sin a big deal? Consider its just punishment: wrath—that holy, overwhelming indignation perfectly suited to almighty God and fixed upon every person (3:23–26). Jesus came to turn away God's wrath. On the cross long ago, the massive, violent force of God's wrath that we deserve struck the Savior instead.

All our sin fell on Jesus, so all our hope rests on Him. Through our faith in Christ, God has a new verdict for us: innocent. Because our Savior's heroic mission of death and resurrection is finished and complete, our attempt to work for God's favor is a ridiculous mockery. We're justified—declared righteous—and we're saved from God's wrath forever.

A violent storm of indignation turns to calm, glassy tranquility . . . peace with God. *Salvation is a gift through faith in Jesus* (3:21–31). Like the old hymn "Jesus! What a Friend for Sinners!" says: "Hallelujah! What a Savior!"

Week 25

Monday: Salvation by Grace through Faith Illustrated
- ☐ *Romans 4*
- ☐ *Psalm 35*

Tuesday: The Contrasting Effects of Two Men
- ☐ *Romans 5*
- ☐ *Psalm 36*

Wednesday: The Potential of Freedom from Sin's Domination
- ☐ *Romans 6*
- ☐ *Psalm 37:1–22*

Thursday: The Reality of the Sinful Nature
- ☐ *Romans 7*
- ☐ *Psalm 37:23–40*

Friday: The Potential of Victory through the Holy Spirit
- ☐ *Romans 8*
- ☐ *Psalm 38*

What I Want to Remember ...

_____

_____

_____

_____

My order of priorities reflects the level of my commitment to Christ. Whoever or whatever is in first place, if it isn't the Lord Jesus, is in the wrong place. Life is like a coin. Spend it any way you wish, but you only spend it once. How are you spending it?

—Charles R. Swindoll

Two Gardens . . . Two Choices . . . Two Results

Anyone can count the seeds in an apple, but only God can count the apples in a seed. Only the Lord knows the staggering potential inside each decision we make.

Two gardens, Eden and Gethsemane, gave stage to two choices that brought opposite results. Adam's choice to sin brought condemnation to all humanity, while Christ's decision to die for sin provided potential justification to all people (Romans 5:18). Adam might have never eaten the fruit had he known the severe consequences his choice would bring to himself and to his race. Jesus's decision in Gethsemane, however, brought immeasurable blessing for humankind.

Like Adam in Eden, we can compromise God's Word in the here and now and live with overwhelming regret. Or, like Jesus in Gethsemane, we can take God at His Word — even when it costs us dearly — knowing the Father makes the potential gain worth the sacrifice.

Our choices can produce good beyond imagination. When a man named Mordecai Ham shared the good news of Jesus Christ to a young boy, he had no idea of the good that would result. Not many people know Ham's name, but through Ham's simple faithfulness, God converted Billy Graham.

Every day we walk in the gardens of decision. Just as Jesus made the hard choice of obedience in the garden for all humanity, so we need to fight the good fight today and choose the long-term benefits that faithfulness offers.[11]

Week 26

Monday: Are You a Child of Promise?
- ☐ Romans 9
- ☐ Psalm 39

Tuesday: Confess and Believe
- ☐ Romans 10
- ☐ Psalm 40

Wednesday: Grafting in the Wild Olives
- ☐ Romans 11
- ☐ Psalm 41

Thursday: We Are Many; We Are One
- ☐ Romans 12
- ☐ Psalm 42

Friday: Be a Good Citizen
- ☐ Romans 13
- ☐ Psalm 43

What I Want to Remember . . .

If we're going to crawl up on an altar and give God our lives as living sacrifices, we have to bring with us our eyes, our ears, our tongues, our hands, and our feet. To carry out Paul's command in Romans 12:1, we have to pay attention to what we look at, what we listen to, what we say, what we do, and where we go.

—Charles R. Swindoll

Everything Is Spiritual

When an Old Testament saint made a sacrifice at the altar, it most often involved taking the life of an animal as an act of devotion toward God. With the coming of Jesus, sacrificing animals at the temple altar was no longer required — Jesus had made the ultimate sacrifice.

However, Jesus's death did not mean that His followers then and now would no longer make sacrifices. Instead of animals, people are to give themselves, following Jesus's sacrificial model and presenting their "bodies a living and holy sacrifice" (Romans 12:1). In the case of martyrdom, such a sacrifice even requires death.

For most Christians, though, the sacrifice takes place day by day, moment by moment, through a myriad of little acts — loving without hypocrisy, contributing to the needs of believers, or being of the same mind toward other believers (12:9–21). How did Paul refer to this life of sacrifice? He called it a "spiritual service of worship" (12:1).

According to the apostle Paul, the lives we lead as Christians are to be inherently oriented toward the sacrifice of worship. But that isn't limited to a church service. Paul envisioned our spiritual lives reflected in our earthly deeds, and vice versa. And this makes sense, for as believers, we carry with us the indwelling Holy Spirit. He is with us in all that we do. Everything is spiritual.

Week 27

Monday: Being Strong in Humility
- ☐ Romans 14
- ☐ Psalm 44

Tuesday: Paul's Personal Travel Plans
- ☐ Romans 15
- ☐ Psalm 45

Wednesday: Paul's Personal Greetings
- ☐ Romans 16
- ☐ Psalm 46

Thursday: Welcome to Corinth . . . and a Contentious Church
- ☐ 1 Corinthians 1
- ☐ Psalm 47

Friday: Striving to Be Spiritual People
- ☐ 1 Corinthians 2
- ☐ Psalm 48

What I Want to Remember . . .

_____

_____

_____

_____

_____

There is an important dimension to hanging tough that you dare not miss. It is the thing that keeps you going. I call it a dream.

—Charles R. Swindoll

Big Dreams, Big God

Paul was about 50 years old when he penned his letter to the Roman Christians. With three missionary journeys under his belt, six books of Scripture to his credit, and thousands of people impassioned for God, Paul held quite a portfolio. If his career had stopped right there, no one would have protested. Many consider age 50 as the time to start coasting toward retirement. But not Paul.

The apostle continued to dream of how he could do more for Christ. He wanted to go to Spain, the western limit of the Roman Empire (Romans 15:24, 28). This represented a big and bold dream. But Paul had a big God.

Life gets fueled on dreams. Without a purpose, we wither and die. As Christians, we have more to do than get up, work hard, and go home for a few hours of television . . . only to rise and begin again. One day, we will wake up and realize life has amounted to a stack of paychecks and a few laughs. God wants more for us than that!

Christ's Great Commission offers us this purpose: "make disciples of all the nations" (Matthew 28:19). Beyond making money, we should purpose to make disciples—in our homes, in our churches, and in our world.

So Paul dreamed of Spain. (Oh, and he wrote seven more New Testament letters.) What's your "Spain"? What's your passion? Do you have a purpose bigger than yourself? Is your dream as big as your God? [12]

Week 28

Monday: Build on the Sure Foundation: Jesus Christ
- [ ] 1 Corinthians 3
- [ ] Psalm 49

Tuesday: Follow the Faithful Servant-Leader
- [ ] 1 Corinthians 4
- [ ] Psalm 50

Wednesday: Do Not Associate with the Immoral Christian
- [ ] 1 Corinthians 5
- [ ] Psalm 51

Thursday: Resolve Conflicts and Flee Sexual Immorality
- [ ] 1 Corinthians 6
- [ ] Psalm 52

Friday: Marriage, Divorce, and Remarriage . . . God's Way
- [ ] 1 Corinthians 7
- [ ] Psalm 53

What I Want to Remember . . .

_____

_____

_____

_____

———— ✔ ————

Sometimes the most responsible thing you can do is warn someone of impending danger. By sounding the alarm, you're not being cantankerous or neurotic. You're not a naysayer. You're a realist. If you know something has potential of bringing harm to others, giving a bold, strong warning is your duty! Not to do so is neglect.

—Charles R. Swindoll

DIFFICULT CONVERSATIONS

No one relishes difficult conversations. In fact, many Christians regularly avoid them. Not Paul. The apostle plainly addressed several "ouch-factor" issues that were hurting the Corinthian church in his day, issues that regularly haunt our own headlines: sex scandals, jealousy, legal squabbles, conflict, and pride. In the face of trying circumstances, Paul did not remain silent. He called the Corinthians "arrogant" (1 Corinthians 5:2), denounced their boastful attitude (5:6), and shed light on their shame (6:5).

Imagine what your home, workplace, or church would be like if no one ever had a difficult conversation. How many people would be on the wrong path, watching TV instead of doing chores, ranting at politicians instead of voting, making excuses instead of serving others? A difficult conversation is often what precipitates change.

The Bible calls believers to "spur one another on to love and good deeds" (Hebrews 10:24 NIV). The word *spur* means "to irritate" or "to prod." When the age-old virtue of stepping-up-to-the-plate is exercised *in love*, it can be a powerful thing. With a whisper, a calm chat, or even an impactful text message, the straying saint can come home, the sideways relationship can be straightened out, and the unmotivated can get moving in the right direction.

Paul refused to take the path of least resistance. He addressed head on the problems among believers. Consider today any difficult conversations you may need to have with others, and imitate Paul in his passion for purity and unity among God's people.

Week 29

Monday: Tough Decisions
- ☐ 1 Corinthians 8
- ☐ Psalm 54

Tuesday: For the Sake of the Gospel
- ☐ 1 Corinthians 9
- ☐ Psalm 55

Wednesday: How to Live for the Glory of God
- ☐ 1 Corinthians 10
- ☐ Psalm 56

Thursday: Remembering the Lord's Death until He Comes
- ☐ 1 Corinthians 11
- ☐ Psalm 57

Friday: How to Help the Body of Christ
- ☐ 1 Corinthians 12
- ☐ Psalm 58

What I Want to Remember . . .

_____

_____

_____

_____

The unsurpassed glory of our God is deserving of our thanks. He didn't lower His standard when He met us at the cross. He didn't change His character when we contaminated our lives with sin. He didn't walk away from us when we were wracked with pain. And He doesn't leave us when we die. All because of His glory.

—Charles R. Swindoll

LIVE FOR GOD'S GLORY

"Whatever you do, do all to the glory of God."

First Corinthians 10:31 gives every follower of Christ a personal mission statement: *I live for God's glory.*

Some elements of all believers' stories are the same. Before we came to Christ, we lived far from God (Romans 3:23). This distance is deadly, but God has a solution: "For the wages of sin is death, but the free gift of God is eternal life in Christ Jesus our Lord" (6:23). Then, because Jesus came near to us and we trusted Him as Savior, God welcomed us near to Himself (Ephesians 2:13).

Now, God's glory is our goal. With the fame of God's name as our ambition, we worry less about what people think and more about what God thinks. We talk less about other people and more about God's greatness. Our perspective moves from horizontal to vertical. Wonderful things happen when we focus on God's glory.

Whether or not we contribute to it, the celebration of God's glory is our future. David caught that grand perspective when he wrote of the day the kings of earth will gather around Jesus on the throne and everyone will sing of God's great glory (Psalm 138:4–5). We don't have to wait for eternity to lift high the glory of God. We must simply acknowledge the greatness of who God is and live like we believe it.

Practice saying your mission statement right now: *I live for God's glory*.

Week 30

Monday: Love above All Virtues
- ☐ 1 Corinthians 13
- ☐ Psalm 59

Tuesday: Gifts for Edifying the Church
- ☐ 1 Corinthians 14
- ☐ Psalm 60

Wednesday: The End of Death and the Hope of Resurrection
- ☐ 1 Corinthians 15
- ☐ Psalm 61

Thursday: Accomplishing the Lord's Work
- ☐ 1 Corinthians 16
- ☐ Psalm 62

Friday: Sharing in Suffering and in Comfort
- ☐ 2 Corinthians 1
- ☐ Psalm 63

What I Want to Remember . . .

_____

_____

_____

_____

How can you best respond to Paul's definition of love in 1 Corinthians 13? Tell the Lord, "I admire these qualities. I want them, but I can't produce them. I'm willing to change in each area, but You, Father, will have to do it through me. Help me to love as You would have me love."

— Charles R. Swindoll

Love Matters

Ask people if they consider themselves "loving," and the far majority will answer in the affirmative. We can quickly marshal evidence in our favor, showing the many ways we display our love to the world. We will even nod our approval when hearing Paul's famous love passage read in our presence (1 Corinthians 13:4–8). But do we really exemplify love?

This vision of love is best revealed by those among us who are the most mature — patient people, kind people, persevering people. Interestingly, in Paul's definition of *love*, he spent more words making clear what love is *not*: jealous, braggadocious, and arrogant, to name a few. Paul also echoed his other letters, mentioning one characteristic that sits at the heart of the others: love does not seek its own (Ephesians 5:21; Philippians 2:4). Love naturally points outward toward others, rather than inward toward ourselves.

Those of us who embrace the love of God lived out in our lives will not brag of our achievements to enhance our own interests. We will not, out of arrogance, force others into a mold that serves our interests. And we will not lie.

In 1 Corinthians 13, Paul laid out a high standard for the people of God. Given our fallen nature, the temptation to cut corners is immense. A close reading of this passage should leave us humbled by our weakness and dependent upon God's grace to empower us to love others as He has loved us.

Week 31

Monday: A Leader's Care for His People
- ☐ 2 Corinthians 2
- ☐ Psalm 64

Tuesday: A Brightly Shining Glory
- ☐ 2 Corinthians 3
- ☐ Psalm 65

Wednesday: Living in God's Power, Not Our Own
- ☐ 2 Corinthians 4
- ☐ Psalm 66

Thursday: New Creatures in Christ
- ☐ 2 Corinthians 5
- ☐ Psalm 67

Friday: Serving the Lord with Distinction
- ☐ 2 Corinthians 6
- ☐ Psalm 68:1–19

What I Want to Remember . . .

_____

_____

_____

_____

In 2 Corinthians, Paul gave us his journal—unedited and unvarnished. He groaned. He wept. He defended. He exposed the truth of his life. He revealed himself for all to see. And he did it in such a self-forgetful way that you walk away shaking your head at the genius of the whole writing.
—*Charles R. Swindoll*

WATCH OVER THOSE IN YOUR CHARGE

Paul had a tenuous relationship with the Corinthian church. This young church struggled profoundly with sin. Letter after letter, Paul wrote strong words of warning about their behavior, no doubt ruffling some feathers in the process.

As Paul wrote 2 Corinthians, he referred to a previous "sorrowful" letter—not 1 Corinthians but another letter that has not been preserved today (2 Corinthians 2:2–3). He was grieved and in anguish over their sin. Like any spiritual mentor, he cared deeply for the people and desired to see them pursue only Christ. Paul understood that the sinful and selfish behavior of even just one person makes a negative impact on the outlook of the whole group. The sins of one believer bring distress, grief, and hurt to other believers (2:5).

Paul's deep love and concern caused him to take action. Leadership demands continual investment in people, if people are to make the greatest possible impact for Christ. For that to occur, it was imperative that Paul both know his people intimately and speak forcefully against sinners on behalf of the whole.

Such was Paul's task in the first century, and it remains ours today. Too many parents and leaders hide from confrontation and avoid the tough talk—leaving sinful people one less avenue for repentance and allowing the group to suffer.

Take action over those in your charge. Show them that you love them by being willing to do the uncomfortable, just like Paul did.

Week 32

Monday: Sorrow That Leads to Repentance
- ☐ 2 Corinthians 7
- ☐ Psalm 68:20–35

Tuesday: Abound in Gracious Works
- ☐ 2 Corinthians 8
- ☐ Psalm 69:1–19

Wednesday: God Loves a Cheerful Giver
- ☐ 2 Corinthians 9
- ☐ Psalm 69:20–36

Thursday: Judging the Image and Not the Substance
- ☐ 2 Corinthians 10
- ☐ Psalm 70

Friday: Guard the Simplicity and Purity of Devotion to Christ
- ☐ 2 Corinthians 11
- ☐ Psalm 71

What I Want to Remember . . .

_____

_____

_____

_____

We find certain words and phrases especially appealing in this age in which we live. How seldom do our adult ears ever hear the phrase, "I am sorry"? How rarely do our own mouths say, "I was wrong and I repent"?

—Charles R. Swindoll

SORROWFUL, THOUGH ONLY FOR A WHILE

We live in a world that avoids sorrow at all costs. The impulse for this can come from a good place. As Christians, our hope is rooted in Christ bringing us into eternity, an existence with no more sorrow (Revelation 21:4). Until then, sin endures; therefore, sorrow endures.

As we have seen, when Paul wrote 2 Corinthians, he had already written the church a tough letter detailing some of their shocking failures — disputes and sexually immoral behavior among believers (1 Corinthians 5–6). Paul's references to these and other sins left the Corinthian believers with "sorrow," a circumstance that Paul, surprisingly, did not regret (2 Corinthians 7:8–13).

The apostle was not interested in pulling the rug out from under the Corinthians' joy — he had a reason for his position. Paul wanted the believers to be "sorrowful to the point of repentance" (7:9). This kind of sorrow — the sorrow that leads Christians to repent of sin — is "according to the will of God" (7:9).

God wants us to be sorrowful? Yes! We need sorrow when we are in the midst of our sin so that we come back to Him. But Paul placed an important barrier around such sorrow: it should lead to repentance "without regret." In other words, as believers, we need not constantly dwell in sorrow and regret. Rather, our sorrow should be of a temporary nature, a sorrow that ends just as soon as we recover our bearings and follow Christ in word and in deed.

Week 33

Monday: The Balance between Boasting and Suffering
- ☐ 2 Corinthians 12
- ☐ Psalm 72

Tuesday: In Our Weakness, God Displays His Power
- ☐ 2 Corinthians 13
- ☐ Psalm 73

Wednesday: The Attack of the Distorted Gospel
- ☐ Galatians 1
- ☐ Psalm 74

Thursday: Peter and Paul Argue over the Gentiles
- ☐ Galatians 2
- ☐ Psalm 75

Friday: Faith in Jesus Christ Brings Righteousness
- ☐ Galatians 3
- ☐ Psalm 76

What I Want to Remember . . .

_____

_____

_____

_____

One of the most serious problems facing the Christian church today is legalism. One of the most serious problems facing the Christian church in Paul's day was legalism. Legalism wrenches the joy of the Lord from the Christian believer, and when the joy of the Lord goes, so does the power He gives us to experience vital worship and vibrant service.

—Charles R. Swindoll

A Different "Gospel"

Everyone likes receiving good news, though reactions differ depending on the content. A child reacts with gratitude over a new toy. A young couple reacts with excitement when they find out they will be parents. And a middle-aged parent reacts with pride (and relief!) when a college-aged child receives a scholarship.

Paul understood this reality about good news, which helps explain his alarm at the disturbing changes occurring in the Galatian church. The apostle knew that if these people who called themselves Christians changed the good news of the gospel, their lives would change dramatically—both then and for eternity.

Paul made clear that though the Galatians were embracing this new message as good news, it actually wasn't (Galatians 1:6–7). They had traded the grace of God that brings faith in Christ for a legalistic life dictated by rules and works. These believers had come under the influence of a group called Judaizers, people who believed that salvation in Christ required following the Mosaic Law.

Without mincing words, the apostle told the Galatians that accepting a message like that of the Judaizers would leave them cursed—separated from God for eternity. The effects of another "gospel" were the same then as they are now: living by law rather than grace undercuts the significance of Jesus's death (2:21) and leads to a joyless pursuit of a Christlike ideal that we can never achieve without God's empowering grace.

Week 34

Monday: Adopted as Sons, Children of Promise
- ☐ Galatians 4
- ☐ Psalm 77

Tuesday: Live According to the Spirit's Direction
- ☐ Galatians 5
- ☐ Psalm 78:1–16

Wednesday: Do Not Lose Heart in Doing Good
- ☐ Galatians 6
- ☐ Psalm 78:17–33

Thursday: The Results of Our Redemption
- ☐ Ephesians 1
- ☐ Psalm 78:34–53

Friday: We Were Dead, but God . . .
- ☐ Ephesians 2
- ☐ Psalm 78:54–72

What I Want to Remember . . .

_____

_____

_____

_____

_____

Without Christ, we are dead. We can't breathe a breath of spiritual air. We can't hear a word of spiritual direction. In His mercy and love, God gives us newness of life.

—Charles R. Swindoll

But God . . .

But God.

So small yet so significant, some have called these the most important six letters in all of Scripture. We tend to over-look the little things in life, and the importance of these two little words is no exception.

Paul began Ephesians 2 commenting on one of the obvious "big" truths of the Bible: human beings are "dead" in our "trespasses and sins" (Ephesians 2:1). As sinful people without Jesus Christ in our lives, we have no spiritual life in us. Our situation, left to our own spiritually dead selves, is hopeless.

But God. God was not content to leave the entire human race to judgment. He sent His Son to die for humanity and raised Him to life, just as He will raise those of us who have placed our faith in Jesus (2:4–5).

The Lord is merciful and loving. And in providing us with life through Jesus Christ, God shows us that mercy and love demand action. We are grateful for God's action on our behalf. In turn, we should show mercy and love toward others.

Have you shared the message of life in Christ with some-one recently? Is there someone you know who needs to hear it? Also, consider how you might show mercy and love in deed rather than word — to believers and unbelievers alike.

It's just a short phrase. But when we dwell upon its mean-ing, *but God* continues to have an eternal impact.

Week 35

Monday: Paul, Steward of God's Grace
- ☐ Ephesians 3
- ☐ Psalm 79

Tuesday: A Unified Body . . .
- ☐ Ephesians 4
- ☐ Psalm 80

Wednesday: . . . Walking in Wisdom
- ☐ Ephesians 5
- ☐ Psalm 81

Thursday: Put On the Armor of God
- ☐ Ephesians 6
- ☐ Psalm 82

Friday: To Live Is Christ; to Die Is Gain
- ☐ Philippians 1
- ☐ Psalm 83

What I Want to Remember . . .

_____

_____

_____

_____

When I became a member of the body of Christ as a result of faith in the Lord Jesus Christ who died for me on the cross and rose from the grave, I stepped into the realm of unity that He established. That's what He wants for His body of believers.

—Charles R. Swindoll

Preserve the Bond of Peace

We've all witnessed or even participated in fights—physical bouts or verbal wars that leave the participants scarred or, worse, at continued odds with one another. Disunity resulting from conflict is bad enough on its own—but when it occurs among believers, it becomes an even greater tragedy.

Ministering to Christians in churches in the Mediterranean world, the apostle Paul was keenly aware of the toll that disunity takes on God's people. He also knew how contrary disunity is to God's nature, message, and purpose in the world. He made it clear to the Ephesians that there is only "one Lord, one faith, one baptism, [and] one God and Father of all" (Ephesians 4:5–6). The very essence of the Christian faith demands unity.

One Jesus and one gospel demands oneness, or unity—not uniformity or unanimity—in the body of Christ. Peace matters because when we dwell in disunity, it's as if we are breaking Christ into pieces of our own making. We undermine God's mission in the world when we allow disunity in the church body. We also place ourselves at risk, eschewing the opportunity to grow in maturity and to benefit from the gifts of people we have cut out of our lives.

Are you creating or supporting unity among believers? Are you making *every effort* to preserve the "bond of peace" (4:3), with humility, gentleness, and tolerance for others (4:2)? In these efforts, we illustrate our commitment to our one God, one Lord, and one Spirit.

Week 36

Monday: Follow God's Humble Servant
- ☐ *Philippians 2*
- ☐ *Psalm 84*

Tuesday: Live as Citizens of Heaven
- ☐ *Philippians 3*
- ☐ *Psalm 85*

Wednesday: Rejoice! The Peace and Grace of God
- ☐ *Philippians 4*
- ☐ *Psalm 86*

Thursday: Jesus Christ: The Image of the Invisible God
- ☐ *Colossians 1*
- ☐ *Psalm 87*

Friday: Jesus Makes Us Complete
- ☐ *Colossians 2*
- ☐ *Psalm 88*

What I Want to Remember . . .

_____

_____

_____

_____

In the day in which we live, how many people do you know of who model a Christlike attitude? Precious few. Ours is a day marked by looking out for number one, by maintaining, defending and, if necessary, pursuing one's own rights.

— Charles R. Swindoll

THE HUMBLING CROSS

The cross sits at the center of the Christian understanding of salvation. We cannot conceive of "being saved" without the instrumental work that Jesus did on the cross. But does the cross apply only to salvation? Might it also apply to sanctification — growing holy in the Christian life?

In Philippians 2, Paul made a strong connection between the cross and the Christian life. He called on the Philippian believers to humbly "regard one another as more important than yourselves" (Philippians 2:3). Paul exhorted Christians to set aside selfishness and look out for the interests of others. The idea here is not that we think of ourselves as pieces of garbage or doormats for others to walk upon, but that we act first out of consideration for others, rather than for ourselves.

Paul's model for this kind of living is none other than Jesus Himself. We are to take on the attitude of Christ, who "humbled Himself by becoming obedient to the point of death" (2:8). Considering the needs of others before our own does not come naturally, because it means undergoing a kind of death as we set aside competing desires for our own fulfillment and focus our attentions outward on others.

The cross is not merely the centerpiece of Christian salvation. Paul made clear it should also be the centerpiece of the Christian life.

Take a moment and consider: how else might the cross inform how you live your life today?

Week 37

Monday: Do Everything with Jesus in Mind
- ☐ *Colossians 3*
- ☐ *Psalm 89:1–18*

Tuesday: Practical Instructions for Everyday Life
- ☐ *Colossians 4*
- ☐ *Psalm 89:19–37*

Wednesday: The Good Example of Faithful Believers
- ☐ *1 Thessalonians 1*
- ☐ *Psalm 89:38–52*

Thursday: Living for Christ in Spite of Suffering
- ☐ *1 Thessalonians 2*
- ☐ *Psalm 90*

Friday: The Results of Faith: Comfort and Joy
- ☐ *1 Thessalonians 3*
- ☐ *Psalm 91*

What I Want to Remember . . .

_____

_____

_____

_____

Play an instrument? Do it in the name of the Jesus. Work at an occupation that takes a lot of patience? Do it in the name of Jesus. It'll take the grind out of it. Tend the home, raising kids? Do it in the name of Jesus. It'll revolutionize your whole concept of life.

—Charles R. Swindoll

Just as Good as Advertised

In the modern world, we have grown accustomed to the omnipresence of advertising. What's more, we understand that most products are never quite as good as advertised—that new shampoo is most definitely *not* the first step to becoming a new you.

The Bible provides the real portrait of "the new you." Paul's words remind believers that in coming to faith in Christ, we have "put on the new self who is being renewed to a true knowledge according to the image of the One who created him" (Colossians 3:10).

While "the new self" is our true identity, we don't always live that way. The path to embodying that new self begins by understanding God's goal for us: that we live in a way that mirrors the life of Jesus. With this in mind, Paul made a number of practical exhortations throughout this passage. He outlined negative behaviors to avoid: anger, wrath, malice, slander, abusive speech, and lies. He also covered positive behaviors to pursue: compassion, kindness, humility, gentleness, patience, forgiveness, and love (3:8–14).

Paul summarized this life as a new person by writing that Christians are to do all things in the name of Jesus (3:17). In other words, all our deeds should be characterized by qualities such as those he listed.

The lives that result will be a constant reminder to others that Christianity is just as good as advertised.

Week 38

Monday: The Christian Walk—Distinctive in Life,
        Triumphant in Death
- ☐ *1 Thessalonians 4*
- ☐ *Psalm 92*

Tuesday: The Christian Walk—Like Day against the
        World's Night
- ☐ *1 Thessalonians 5*
- ☐ *Psalm 93*

Wednesday: Hold On—Vindication and Justice Are on
        God's Timetable
- ☐ *2 Thessalonians 1*
- ☐ *Psalm 94*

Thursday: Stand Firm—Deception and Rebellion Are on the
        Enemy's Timetable
- ☐ *2 Thessalonians 2*
- ☐ *Psalm 95*

Friday: Carry On—Be Dignified and Industrious until the
        Lord's Return
- ☐ *2 Thessalonians 3*
- ☐ *Psalm 96*

What I Want to Remember . . .

_____

_____

_____

Look at your trial as God looks at it, and draw upon His power to hold up under the blast. Stand still . . . and refuse to retreat.

—Charles R. Swindoll

FULL OF YEARS, FULL OF JOY, FULL OF LIFE WELL SPENT

One of the greatest privileges we can enjoy is attending the funeral of an old saint. You know the kind: a person full of years, full of joy, full of life well spent. There is generally a richness in the stories you hear from the family members. Of course the bereaved grieve, but their tales are told with a certain joy, a certain enthusiasm. Their recollections are woven with *hope*. And that makes all the difference. They have not only the memories of times gone by but confidence in times to come as well.

Death is no fearsome curse for the Christian; rather, it announces the consummation of new life. Knowing this frees us to celebrate the earthly life of the departed, even if it was modest and ordinary . . . even if it was, in fact, difficult.

The kind of Christian life that Paul called excellent is really quite unremarkable by worldly estimations. But it's the sort of life we remember fondly at its ending—modest, dignified, and industrious (1 Thessalonians 4:11–12). Even the great "movers and shakers" of the faith want to be remembered this way . . . if their faith is true.

Are you walking through life with your own funeral in mind? When people gather, will they grieve as if there is no hope, or will they celebrate a life full of joy—a life well spent?

Week 39

Monday: The Value of Sound Doctrine
- ☐ 1 Timothy 1
- ☐ Psalm 97

Tuesday: The Key to a Quiet and Tranquil Life
- ☐ 1 Timothy 2
- ☐ Psalm 98

Wednesday: Qualifications for the Church's Leaders
- ☐ 1 Timothy 3
- ☐ Psalm 99

Thursday: Lead a Disciplined Life
- ☐ 1 Timothy 4
- ☐ Psalm 100

Friday: Take Proper Care of Widows
- ☐ 1 Timothy 5
- ☐ Psalm 101

What I Want to Remember . . .

_____

_____

_____

_____

Let me offer a word about a concept that isn't in vogue in our twenty-first century: discipline. I have never seen anyone automatically become godly. Discipline doesn't work like that. It isn't easy, it isn't quick, and frankly, it isn't without pain. In order to achieve what you want, it is essential that a price be paid.

—*Charles R. Swindoll*

Exercising the Body and the Soul

Most people have accepted the value of regular physical exercise—if we aren't doing it, we know we should be. We appreciate exercise in part for its health benefits. But it is also one of the ways we can practice discipline in our lives. Through the training of the body, just as in other physical practices like fasting from food or denying ourselves some other earthly good, we become more disciplined people.

On a cursory reading, the apostle Paul seemed to undercut the value of physical discipline when he said that "bodily discipline is only of little profit" (1 Timothy 4:8). However, when we read his clear commitment to physical discipline in 1 Corinthians 9:27, we can see that Paul's purpose in 1 Timothy was not to lead Timothy to ignore all manner of physical regimens. Instead, Paul wanted the young pastor to remember that physical practices and disciplines on their own do not equate godliness.

A physically disciplined person is not necessarily a godly person, but as believers, we can use the practice of physical discipline to prepare ourselves to be disciplined in our spiritual lives. In this light, both physical and spiritual discipline have value in our lives. Ultimately though, our discipline in the spiritual realm prevails. It reflects the hope that we have in the life to come—"godliness is profitable for all things" (1 Timothy 4:8).

The physically strong are common, but their strength has limited effects. The spiritually strong are rare, but their strength has abundant impact.

Week 40

Monday: Fighting the Good Fight of Faith
- ☐ 1 Timothy 6
- ☐ Psalm 102

Tuesday: The Power of Deep Spiritual Roots
- ☐ 2 Timothy 1
- ☐ Psalm 103

Wednesday: How to be a Solider and a Worker for Christ
- ☐ 2 Timothy 2
- ☐ Psalm 104:1–17

Thursday: Watching Out for Evil People
- ☐ 2 Timothy 3
- ☐ Psalm 104:18–35

Friday: Finish Strong . . . Finish Well
- ☐ 2 Timothy 4
- ☐ Psalm 105:1–24

What I Want to Remember . . .

_____

_____

_____

_____

No one I know has endured the level of hardship Paul did as a good soldier of Christ. Yet, never once did he give a hint of complaint for being chained to a burly Roman soldier or inconvenienced by confining, cramped quarters. He simply would not grumble. By God's grace, he had learned the secret of contentment.

—Charles R. Swindoll

Passing the Baton

If anyone had a right to express discontent, it was Paul.

Isolated in a clammy Roman prison, he had ample time to reflect on his years of hard-fought ministry—the good, the bad, and the unfinished. Surely he was tempted at times to let his disappointments overshadow his joyful memories of doing God's work. After all, he was only human.

Yet when he wrote his second letter to his young charge Timothy, Paul was feeling anything but disgruntled. Despite the fact that some church folks had let him down, Paul continued to let God invigorate his spirit.

Why? Timothy was on his mind. Paul understood the value of imparting wisdom to this fresh-faced protégé. After telling Timothy to "fight the good fight" (1 Timothy 6:12), Paul changed his focus in the second letter, saying he, Paul, had "fought the good fight . . . finished the course . . . [and] kept the faith" (2 Timothy 4:7). With death on his doorstep, Paul used his own life as an example for Timothy of how to persevere in ministry with vitality.

Paul truly understood how to bloom where he was planted—even if that meant in a dark prison. His emphatic encouragement reminds us that, if we look around, there are others like Timothy—willing yet vulnerable warriors of the faith—who could use a little push.

Whom can you encourage today?

Week 41

Monday: Hold Fast to God's Word
- ☐ Titus 1
- ☐ Psalm 105:25–45

Tuesday: Let the Older Teach the Younger
- ☐ Titus 2
- ☐ Psalm 106:1–15

Wednesday: Christian, Engage in Good Deeds
- ☐ Titus 3
- ☐ Psalm 106:16–31

Thursday: A Plea for a Slave
- ☐ Philemon 1
- ☐ Psalm 106:32–48

Friday: The Centrality of God's Son
- ☐ Hebrews 1
- ☐ Psalm 107:1–16

What I Want to Remember . . .

_____

_____

_____

The world of the first century was just as unabashedly impure as ours is today—except for one thing: the church was pure. That doesn't mean only perfect people were there. It means Christians maintained a sense of purity, a hard-line position that they would live in such a way to make themselves distinct. How else was anyone to tell the difference between the church and the world?

—Charles R. Swindoll

Pure Heart, Pure Life

When Jesus sat with sinners and tax collectors, the ritually "pure" Pharisees looked down their noses and whispered in disapproval and disgust (Mark 2:15–17). Jesus was, for the most part, unconcerned, understanding His mission as one to all people in need of help. Surrounding Himself with the impure for the sake of ministry actually enhanced and completed His mission, rather than compromised it.

In the letter to Titus, Paul taught that "to the pure, all things are pure" (Titus 1:15). The apostle wrote here not of the ritualistic purity of the Pharisees, a purity that went only skin deep. Instead, he referred to those who were pure in heart, those whose purity extended to every aspect of their beings, whose purity dictated how they thought and behaved.

For those whose hearts have been purified — believers whose hearts have been made pure — "all things are pure." On a basic level, this simply means that no dietary restriction made a person clean or unclean; Jesus had taught as much (Mark 7:15). But the broader principle of purity extends to *all* behavior — not just to eating.

Christians should be interacting with the world around us from a place of purity. In other words, God has purified us from our sin. Therefore, our behavior should be pure as well.

God has a particular way He wants His people to conduct themselves in the world. As we follow that way, we will change our approach to everything and everyone in the world — not interacting with the world out of fear of our contamination but rather out of hope for its renewal.

Week 42

Monday: Our Merciful and Faithful High Priest
- [ ] Hebrews 2
- [ ] Psalm 107:17–32

Tuesday: Become a Partaker of Christ
- [ ] Hebrews 3
- [ ] Psalm 107:33–43

Wednesday: Rest for Those Who Believe
- [ ] Hebrews 4
- [ ] Psalm 108

Thursday: The Perfect Source of Eternal Salvation
- [ ] Hebrews 5
- [ ] Psalm 109

Friday: Take Hold of the Hope Set before Us
- [ ] Hebrews 6
- [ ] Psalm 110

What I Want to Remember . . .

_____

_____

_____

_____

Obedience calls for unselfishness. You will find yourself faced eyeball-to-eyeball with what you know underneath to be the will of God, and it will not please you. And that's when the bills come due, when you do what you know God would have you do and it doesn't please you.

—Charles R. Swindoll

LEARNING TO OBEY

Just before Jesus ascended to heaven, He told His apostles to make disciples, "teaching them to obey everything" that Jesus had commanded (Matthew 28:20 NIV). His words extend to disciples today. But how do we learn such a lesson? How do we learn to obey?

The writer to the Hebrews offered a clear answer to this question, one rooted in the life and practice of Jesus Himself. After a reference to Christ's prayer for mercy in the garden of Gethsemane, Hebrews 5:8 notes that Jesus "learned obedience from the things which He suffered." This doesn't mean that Jesus, through suffering, exchanged disobedience for obedience. Rather, it was more like a move from innocence to virtue. Obedience through suffering served as Jesus's teacher in virtue. Jesus grew to embody virtue in its fullest sense. He gained this quality through the experience of suffering. Because Christians are followers of Jesus, this is a path He has cut for us as well.

What does learning obedience through suffering mean in the context of how we think about our lives? Could it be that the Christian's life is to be characterized more by suffering from self-denial than by celebration through self-fulfillment? Could it be that the mature Christian is one who regularly obeys in the midst of suffering rather than one who regularly falters in the midst of comforts?

Look for opportunities to learn obedience as Jesus did. Make obedience, rather than avoidance, your first thought in the midst of a trial.

Week 43

Monday: Draw Near to God through a Better Hope
- [ ] *Hebrews 7*
- [ ] *Psalm 111*

Tuesday: Better Ministry, Better Covenant, Better Promises
- [ ] *Hebrews 8*
- [ ] *Psalm 112*

Wednesday: Death and Judgment Covered by Christ
- [ ] *Hebrews 9*
- [ ] *Psalm 113*

Thursday: Hold Fast to the Confession of Our Hope
- [ ] *Hebrews 10*
- [ ] *Psalm 114*

Friday: You've Got to Have Faith
- [ ] *Hebrews 11*
- [ ] *Psalm 115*

What I Want to Remember . . .

_____

_____

_____

_____

The carnal Christian not only is not growing but is not interested in growing. He wants to be entertained. He wants a light diet of milk when he cries for it. He wants his way. And he's going to get it, no matter how many he will have to disrupt.

—Charles R. Swindoll

A Terrifying Judgment

In this age of "I'm okay, you're okay," Christians have all too often ignored the "bad news" of judgment we find in Scripture. But, under the authority of the inspired Word of God, passages on God's judgment are just as vital as those on His love, grace, and mercy. We need to deal with them equally.

Hebrews 10 offers one of the most frank assessments of judgment in Scripture: continual, willful sin by those who have accepted Christ has dangerous, even frightening consequences. Those who have embraced the truth of the gospel yet follow their own path of sin and rebellion can expect the terrifying weight of judgment to bear down upon them (Hebrews 10:26–27). Sin can bring with it both internal and external suffering—internal because of guilt from the act itself and external because of the consequences that come from practicing evil deeds.

The choice to live in continual sin illustrates the condition of the heart, what the writer to the Hebrews called trampling "under foot the Son of God" (10:29). For those who treat Christ in this way, terrifying judgment awaits (10:30–31).

For the Christian, the application of this truth is obvious: it should spur our efforts to persuade our brothers and sisters to follow Jesus faithfully. For only then will they find relief from the suffering that comes with a life of habitual sin.

Week 44

Monday: Is God's Discipline Good?
- [ ] *Hebrews 12*
- [ ] *Psalm 116*

Tuesday: Practical Instruction in Following Jesus
- [ ] *Hebrews 13*
- [ ] *Psalm 117*

Wednesday: Temptations and Trials for the Faithful
- [ ] *James 1*
- [ ] *Psalm 118*

Thursday: Don't Play Favorites
- [ ] *James 2*
- [ ] *Psalm 119:1–16*

Friday: Prodigious Power, Minuscule Muscle
- [ ] *James 3*
- [ ] *Psalm 119:17–32*

What I Want to Remember . . .

_____

_____

_____

_____

Hospitality means showing affection to strangers. When the writer of Hebrews commands hospitality, he tells us to greet the visitors. Do you know what this cuts against? Our prejudice. As Christians, no longer do we shun outsiders, those not "our kind."

—*Charles R. Swindoll*

One Is a Lonely Number

Seventeenth-century poet John Donne famously said that no one is an island. Much as we may want to consider ourselves self-sufficient, God made human beings to live in community with one another. We are to be connected with one another, to work with and love one another (1 Corinthians 12:14–27).

Part of following Christ means going against the individualist trends of the modern world. The Bible regularly mentions the importance of hospitality, even devoting an entire book to the practice (3 John).

Hebrews 13:2 also makes mention of hospitality—which specifically refers to entertaining strangers. At the time of the book's writing, the command meant much more than merely inviting someone over for dinner. In the ancient world, enjoying a meal with a stranger indicated the beginning of a potential lifelong friendship. The ancients recognized the godlike qualities inherent in providing sustenance for others, whether in the form of food, shelter, or meeting some other fundamental need. When the early Christians practiced hospitality, they did so knowing they were imitating God's love and care for His creation.

Do you consider yourself a hospitable person? What are some ways you can show hospitality in your current context? If we Christians do not practice hospitality for others in our homes and from our own provisions, we lose a significant opportunity to show others God's tender love and care.

Week 45

Monday: Surrendering Selfish Desires
- [ ] James 4
- [ ] Psalm 119:33–48

Tuesday: The Lord's Coming: A Reason for Patience
- [ ] James 5
- [ ] Psalm 119:49–64

Wednesday: A Living Hope . . . A Holy Life
- [ ] 1 Peter 1
- [ ] Psalm 119:65–80

Thursday: Submission When Authorities Are Unjust
- [ ] 1 Peter 2
- [ ] Psalm 119:81–96

Friday: Suffering in Marriage and in Life in General
- [ ] 1 Peter 3
- [ ] Psalm 119:97–112

What I Want to Remember . . .

_____

_____

_____

_____

Christians are transplanted aliens. When we came to know Christ, our permanent address changed to heaven. And so we're strangers, pilgrims in a world occupied by and under the domination of someone other than our Master. I get homesick at times and so do you, but we still are here. We're to carry out a job.

—Charles R. Swindoll

OUR REAL HOME

Peter addressed his first letter to the Christians living in the Roman provinces of Asia Minor (1 Peter 1:1). Roman authorities cataloged these Christians as "resident aliens" and considered them second-class citizens. They were allowed to work the land but not own it, forced to join the Roman army and pay taxes but unable to vote or hold public office. This inferior status, brought on by disdain for Christians' different religious beliefs, produced hostility, suspicion, and contempt within the communities where they lived.

While the world viewed these Christians as resident aliens, Peter told them that God viewed them as aliens of another sort. God saw them as people of great worth—chosen, sanctified, and forgiven (1:1–6)—not as second-class. They were great in the eyes of God but less than average in the eyes of the world.

Peter described a tension Christians still feel today. We struggle with living among the hostility and temptations of the world as we cling to the assurance that the God who chose us also loves us more than we can possibly imagine. Our peace comes from knowing that while the world sees us as strange, we are not strangers to God. Our mailboxes may have our names on them, but our real home is somewhere else (Philippians 3:20; 1 Peter 1:1; 2:11).

Our brief trials on earth cannot compare to heaven's eternal joys (Romans 8:18; 1 Peter 1:13).[13]

Week 46

Monday: Suffer According to the Will of God
- ☐ *1 Peter 4*
- ☐ *Psalm 119:113–128*

Tuesday: Serve God's People by Setting a Good Example
- ☐ *1 Peter 5*
- ☐ *Psalm 119:129–144*

Wednesday: How to Be Useful and Fruitful
- ☐ *2 Peter 1*
- ☐ *Psalm 119:145–160*

Thursday: God Judges Those Who Oppose Him
- ☐ *2 Peter 2*
- ☐ *Psalm 119:161–176*

Friday: After Judgment, Renewal
- ☐ *2 Peter 3*
- ☐ *Psalm 120*

What I Want to Remember . . .

_____

_____

_____

_____

_____

If you want to live a useful and fruitful life, 2 Peter 1 is a wonderful place to start. The traits Peter listed are worth your time, your attention, and your effort.

—Charles R. Swindoll

A LIFETIME OF PROGRESS

Often called an era of progress, the last two centuries have seen individuals, nations, science, and the arts move into realms never before heard of in human history. Technological advances like the automobile, the space program, and the Internet altered our perceptions about what was possible in this world. And then our ideas about personal progress changed too. People began to think in terms of bigger bank accounts, higher standards of living, and better medical treatments.

However, when the Bible mentions progress in a personal sense, the focus is internal rather than external, pointing believers forward to what Peter referred to as our becoming "partakers of the divine nature" (2 Peter 1:4). In other words, we should expect to demonstrate godly qualities in every aspect of our beings.

The apostle went on to define in more concrete terms what a godly person looks like. Beginning with faith, which sets believers apart from all other people, Peter added seven qualities that God's people should pursue fervently: moral excellence, knowledge, self-control, perseverance, godliness, brotherly kindness, and love (1:5–7).

This list and our need to pursue it illustrate the need for an active faith—one that recognizes the danger of corruption from sin and the need to progress beyond it. The qualities in Peter's list necessitate action, requiring from us a lifetime of deeds that demonstrate the reality of each of these seven qualities in our hearts.

Week 47

Monday: Love from Above
- ☐ 1 John 1
- ☐ Psalm 121

Tuesday: Love Not the World
- ☐ 1 John 2
- ☐ Psalm 122

Wednesday: Love One Another
- ☐ 1 John 3
- ☐ Psalm 123

Thursday: Love Is from God
- ☐ 1 John 4
- ☐ Psalm 124

Friday: Love Equals Obedience
- ☐ 1 John 5
- ☐ Psalm 125

What I Want to Remember . . .

_____

_____

_____

_____

_____

There is no way on earth that we, in our human flesh, can live this kind of a love life apart from God—no way. We just aren't built like that.

—Charles R. Swindoll

Love: The Essential Ingredient

Is love an essential ingredient in the mature Christian life? Well, let's see. Other than reaching out to a neighbor, praying for a rebellious child, and forgiving a bitter spouse, love is pretty much useless. And, oh. Without it, you don't truly know God.

Indeed, the apostle John wrote that "everyone who loves has been born of God and knows God. Whoever does not love does not know God, because God is love" (1 John 4:7–8 NIV). In other words, love is essential for maturity!

At the beginning of 1 John, the aging apostle summed up his purpose for writing his letter: "So that you too may have fellowship with us; and indeed our fellowship is with the Father, and with His Son Jesus Christ" (1:3). What John recognized is that our communion with the Lord and with others is essential to our faith.

But when we face a bitter family member or a nosy coworker, loving one another seems impossible and sometimes even pointless. Will we love that person as Christ would? Or will we let our emotions tell us how to react? With the help of the Holy Spirit, we *can* choose to respond the right way. In the end, practicing love is more about the choices and commitments we make — beginning with our commitment to the Lord — than the feelings that overwhelm our hearts.

Let's make sure that whomever we talk to, wherever we go, and whatever we do, we always remember to add love: the essential ingredient.

Week 48

Monday: Something Old, Something New
- ☐ 2 John 1
- ☐ Psalm 126

Tuesday: Have God, Will Travel
- ☐ 3 John 1
- ☐ Psalm 127

Wednesday: You Can Start to Make It Better
- ☐ Jude 1
- ☐ Psalm 128

Thursday: Jesus Appears to John
- ☐ Revelation 1
- ☐ Psalm 129

Friday: Your First Love
- ☐ Revelation 2
- ☐ Psalm 130

What I Want to Remember . . .

_____

_____

_____

No one suddenly wakes up and says, "I don't love Jesus anymore." No, it happens little by little over years . . . after hardship, unanswered questions, and trials that don't seem to have reason . . . after lost health, lost hope, and lost loved ones. If your love has cooled off, repent. Turn your course. Take responsibility. Acknowledge your part. The Lord hasn't moved.

—Charles R. Swindoll

Deeds, Doctrine, and Devotion

Thirty years after Paul wrote his letters to the church at Ephesus and to their pastor, Timothy, the Holy Spirit inspired John to write another letter to them. Within the book of Revelation, Jesus highly commended the Ephesians in both their deeds and their doctrine. They labored even to the point of suffering for Christ's name. They put people to the test, preserving sound doctrine. What a church! But Jesus added, "I have this against you . . ." (Revelation 2:4). Really? A complaint?

If Jesus told us today He had a complaint against us, we might pull out our good-deeds checklist and work our way down it. "Should I go on a mission trip? Should I pray more? Should I memorize the book of Romans?"

But Jesus told the Ephesians, "You have left your first love" (2:4). *Ouch.*

Although we passionately serve the Lord and remain firm in our doctrine, like the Ephesians, we can easily let our devotion slip. Our serving Christ should never replace our love for Him (John 15:5). Instead, our devotion should fuel our service . . . and every other activity.

When we first came to Christ, all we had was Him — and He was all we needed. Have we grown so much in knowledge and responsibilities that our love for Jesus has grown cold? Has the Great Commission replaced the great commandment (Matthew 22:36 – 38)?

Let's remember that our deeds and our doctrine need to remain part of — never separate from — our devotion.[14]

Week 49

Monday: Letters to Three Churches
- ☐ Revelation 3
- ☐ Psalm 131

Tuesday: A Scene from the Throne Room
- ☐ Revelation 4
- ☐ Psalm 132

Wednesday: All Eyes on the Lamb That Was Slain
- ☐ Revelation 5
- ☐ Psalm 133

Thursday: Opening the First Six Seal Judgments
- ☐ Revelation 6
- ☐ Psalm 134

Friday: Jews and Gentiles Saved During the Tribulation
- ☐ Revelation 7
- ☐ Psalm 135

What I Want to Remember . . .

_____

_____

_____

Mercy is God's inexhaustible compassion through which He provides infinite relief. It isn't a passive pity. It isn't simply an understanding of our plight. Mercy is not mere sorrow. Mercy is an active force on behalf of offenders, on behalf of victims, whereby He brings relief on purpose. It is grace that helps the helpless. It is mercy that ministers to the miserable.

—*Charles R. Swindoll*

THE MERCY AMIDST THE MAYHEM

Sometimes, we see our lives in all-or-nothing terms—some seasons yield feasts of historic proportions while other seasons languish in famine. Sometimes, though, life is more complex than that.

When God begins to pour out His wrath in judgment on His creation as pictured in Revelation 6, we tend to think of it in purely negative terms. And for good reason—war, famine, death, martyrdom, and ongoing terror are in store for those living when this tribulation period begins.

However, we need not consider the as-yet future tribulation period as a time of judgment alone. For even then, amidst the darkest moments this world will ever see, God's mercy to humanity will shine through. On the heels of introducing the seal judgments in the tribulation, John described a small number of Jews who will be saved from death and destruction (Revelation 7:4). And immediately following this vision of Jewish salvation, John saw a great multitude of believers who came through the tribulation (7:10–14).

These believers remind us that even in the darkest of times, God's offer of help and salvation goes out to His creation. When your life seems most difficult, remember that until the final judgment after the tribulation, God is *always* merciful, inviting us to follow Him and trust in His plan to redeem us from sin and its consequences.

Week 50

Monday: The Seventh Seal Initiates the Trumpet Judgments
- ☐ *Revelation 8*
- ☐ *Psalm 136*

Tuesday: Unrepentant Humanity Tormented and Killed
- ☐ *Revelation 9*
- ☐ *Psalm 137*

Wednesday: John Confirms the Prophecy of Things to Come
- ☐ *Revelation 10*
- ☐ *Psalm 138*

Thursday: Two Witnesses Speak the Truth
- ☐ *Revelation 11*
- ☐ *Psalm 139*

Friday: A Woman, a Dragon, a Child, and an Angel
- ☐ *Revelation 12*
- ☐ *Psalm 140*

What I Want to Remember . . .

_____

_____

_____

_____

Much in the supernatural world is beyond our comprehension; we can't even grasp the dimensions of it. But we, as simple human beings with souls that will last eternally, reaffirm our faith in Christ, our confidence in the cross, and our gratitude for His powerful ability to deliver us from sin and judgment.

—*Charles R. Swindoll*

A Sense of Urgency

Whether it's a child's sports schedule or putting in extra hours at the office, any number of things can cause Scripture's important teachings to blend into the background of our lives. Busyness saps our urgency for significant work. Forgetfulness puts that work out of mind.

One of the most forgotten—or ignored—truths of the Bible is the devastating nature of God's judgment. Judgment occurs throughout the Bible, though one popular (and incorrect) opinion suggests that judgment was a quality of God in the Old Testament but not in the New.

No book of the New Testament encapsulates God's judgment in more striking and vivid terms than Revelation. Earthquakes, sores, fires, and wars, John's vision of the future presents a terrifying portrait of God's judgment on sinful people. One prophecy, found in Revelation 9:1–12, describes locusts from a bottomless pit sent by a fallen angel king to torment humanity for five months (Revelation 9:1–12). These are not just any locusts—this army of judgment has the look of horses, faces like that of men, hair like that of women, and lion's teeth. And they are not creatures from a science-fiction movie. They are real.

The horror of this vision should jolt even the busiest and most forgetful among us out of our ruts. A time of terrible judgment awaits those who have not confessed Jesus Christ as Savior, and our responsibility is to make sure they know. May these scenes of judgment encourage you in your commission as Christ's follower to make disciples, just as He did (Matthew 28:19–20).

Week 51

Monday: The Antichrist and the False Prophet
- ☐ Revelation 13
- ☐ Psalm 141

Tuesday: Triumphant Saints and Victorious Announcements
- ☐ Revelation 14
- ☐ Psalm 142

Wednesday: Heavenly Joy in Advance of Earthly Dread
- ☐ Revelation 15
- ☐ Psalm 143

Thursday: The Bowls of God's Terrible Wrath
- ☐ Revelation 16
- ☐ Psalm 144

Friday: Worldly Religion Destroyed
- ☐ Revelation 17
- ☐ Psalm 145

What I Want to Remember . . .

_____

_____

_____

_____

God takes full responsibility for this world, including the judgment to come. From start to finish, it is all about Him. He misses nothing. He cares about those who are whole and attractive and what we call the beautiful people, just as much as He cares about the broken and the leftovers and the nobodies.

—Charles R. Swindoll

Joy over Judgment

Go to virtually any courtroom sentencing hearing in the world, even for the most vicious criminals, and you will find people disagreeing over the judgment. Some will celebrate that justice has been served, while others lament a missed opportunity.

Regardless of the circumstance, any act of justice this side of God's final judgment will carry with it a tension — one that recognizes both the divine goodness of justice as well as the presence of fallen human beings in delivering the act of justice.

One day in the future, God will bring His plan to completion, a plan that includes levying perfect judgment on those who have not followed Him. We see Him exemplify this in small ways throughout Scripture, most notably in the judgment of the Egyptians at the time of the Exodus (Exodus 14:13–15:21). At that time, because the judgment was so clearly by the hand of God, God's people celebrated His perfect justice.

When the Lord initiates His final judgment on humanity, believers in Christ will recognize the purity of His justice. And we will celebrate, echoing the song of Moses as God once and for all triumphs over His enemies (Revelation 15:1–4).

Pure joy over judgment sounds strange now, but in that glorious day when God makes all things right, it will be a sweet song indeed.

Week 52

Monday: The Demise of All Things Worldly
- [ ] *Revelation 18*
- [ ] *Psalm 146*

Tuesday: The Second Coming of Christ
- [ ] *Revelation 19*
- [ ] *Psalm 147*

Wednesday: Christ's Millennial Kingdom and Great White Throne Judgment
- [ ] *Revelation 20*
- [ ] *Psalm 148*

Thursday: The New Jerusalem Described
- [ ] *Revelation 21*
- [ ] *Psalm 149*

Friday: Our Eternal Bliss and Jesus's Promise to Come
- [ ] *Revelation 22*
- [ ] *Psalm 150*

What I Want to Remember . . .

_____

_____

_____

How in the world do you describe the inevitable sights and sounds of an existence beyond time and space? The magnificent music of angels, a myriad of voices singing in antiphonal sounds, songs never heard before from the mind of God? The stupendous brilliance of transparent, golden streets, the breathtaking splendor of massive pearl gates?

—Charles R. Swindoll

The End and the Beginning

The Bible begins with God placing the Tree of Life alongside the tree of the forbidden fruit. Thus, the created earth became the arena in which human beings could fulfill their purpose of ruling under God . . . for God's glory.

The fall of humanity into sin cursed not only all people but also all creation (Genesis 3:17; Romans 8:20–22). The Old Testament ends not far from its beginning, clutching a hope of redemption from the curse (Malachi 4:5–6).

And the New Testament unveils the solution. The coming of Jesus Christ provided the ultimate endorsement of humanity and blessing of the earth. Jesus revealed the dignity of humanity by becoming human — eternally. While on earth, Jesus fulfilled humanity's original purpose of demonstrating God's glory by living an obedient life — obedient even to death on a cross. Through His atoning sacrifice and resurrection, Jesus removed the curse, providing all people with the opportunity to "eat the fruit from the tree of life" — just as it was in the beginning (Revelation 22:14 NLT).

From the first chapter of the Bible to the last, God used the physical earth as the stage for humanity's spiritual life. The new heaven and earth will reproduce the same intention as the originals; they will provide a platform for human beings to rule under God. By God's grace, Adam literally will get to rule again.

Let us use the ground beneath our feet for the purpose for which God created it — a place to display His glory.[15]

HOW TO BEGIN A RELATIONSHIP WITH GOD

The New Testament reveals the specific identity of the promised Messiah — our Savior — Jesus, God's own Son. These twenty-seven books track His life and point the way forward in faith for those who wish to follow Him. How can we receive the salvation and new life He offers? How can we have a relationship with Jesus? The Bible marks the path with four essential truths. Let's look at each marker in detail.

Our Spiritual Condition: Totally Depraved

The first truth is rather personal. One look in the mirror of Scripture, and our human condition becomes painfully clear:

> "There is none righteous, not even one;
> There is none who understands,
> There is none who seeks for God;
> All have turned aside, together they have
>   become useless;
> There is none who does good,
> There is not even one." (Romans 3:10–12)

We are all sinners through and through — totally depraved. Now, that doesn't mean we've committed every atrocity known to humankind. We're not as *bad* as we can be, just as *bad off* as we can be. Sin colors all our thoughts, motives, words, and actions.

If you've been around a while, you likely already believe it. Look around. Everything around us bears the smudge marks of our sinful nature. Despite our best efforts to create a perfect world, crime statistics continue to soar, divorce rates keep climbing, and families keep crumbling.

Something has gone terribly wrong in our society and in ourselves—something deadly. Contrary to how the world would repackage it, "me-first" living doesn't equal rugged individuality and freedom; it equals death. As Paul said in his letter to the Romans, "The wages of sin is death" (Romans 6:23)—our spiritual and physical death that comes from God's righteous judgment of our sin, along with all of the emotional and practical effects of this separation that we experience on a daily basis. This brings us to the second marker: God's character.

God's Character: Infinitely Holy

How can God judge us for a sinful state we were born into? Our total depravity is only half the answer. The other half is God's infinite holiness.

The fact that we know things are not as they should be points us to a standard of goodness beyond ourselves. Our sense of injustice in life on this side of eternity implies a perfect standard of justice beyond our reality. That standard and source is God Himself. And God's standard of holiness contrasts starkly with our sinful condition.

Scripture says that "God is Light, and in Him there is no darkness at all" (1 John 1:5). God is absolutely holy—which creates a problem for us. If He is so pure, how can we who are so impure relate to Him?

Perhaps we could try being better people, try to tilt the balance in favor of our good deeds, or seek out methods for self-improvement. Throughout history, people have attempted to live up to God's standard by keeping the Ten Commandments or living by their own code of ethics. Unfortunately, no one can come close to satisfying the demands of God's law.

Romans 3:20 says, "By the works of the Law no flesh will be justified in His sight; for through the Law comes the knowledge of sin."

Our Need: A Substitute

So here we are, sinners by nature and sinners by choice, trying to pull ourselves up by our own bootstraps to attain a relationship with our holy Creator. But every time we try, we fall flat on our faces. We can't live a good enough life to make up for our sin, because God's standard isn't "good enough"—it's *perfection*. And we can't make amends for the offense our sin has created without dying for it.

Who can get us out of this mess?

If someone could live perfectly, honoring God's law, and would bear sin's death penalty for us—in our place—then we would be saved from our predicament. But is there such a person? Thankfully, yes!

Meet your substitute—*Jesus Christ*. He is the One who took death's place for you!

> [God] made [Jesus Christ] who knew no
> sin to be sin on our behalf, so that we might
> become the righteousness of God in Him.
> (2 Corinthians 5:21)

God's Provision: A Savior

God rescued us by sending His Son, Jesus, to die on the cross for our sins (1 John 4:9–10). Jesus was fully human and fully divine (John 1:1, 18), a truth that ensures His understanding of our weaknesses, His power to forgive, and His ability to bridge the gap between God and us (Romans 5:6–11).

In short, we are "justified as a gift by His grace through the redemption which is in Christ Jesus" (Romans 3:24). Two words in this verse bear further explanation: *justified* and *redemption*.

Justification is God's act of mercy, in which He declares righteous the believing sinners while we are still in our sinning state. Justification doesn't mean that God *makes* us righteous, so that we never sin again, rather that He *declares* us righteous—much like a judge pardons a guilty criminal. Because Jesus took our sin upon Himself and suffered our judgment on the cross, God forgives our debt and proclaims us PARDONED.

Redemption is Christ's act of paying the complete price to release us from sin's bondage. God sent His Son to bear His wrath for all of our sins—past, present, and future (Romans 3:24–26; 2 Corinthians 5:21). In humble obedience, Christ willingly endured the shame of the cross for our sake (Mark 10:45; Romans 5:6–8; Philippians 2:8). Christ's death satisfied God's righteous demands. He no longer holds our sins against us, because His own Son paid the penalty for them. We are freed from the slave market of sin, never to be enslaved again!

Placing Your Faith in Christ

These four truths describe how God has provided a way to Himself through Jesus Christ. Because the price has been paid in full by God, we must respond to His free gift of eternal life in total faith and confidence in Him to save us. We must step forward into the relationship with God that He has prepared for us—not by doing good works or by being a good person, but by coming to Him just as we are and accepting His justification and redemption by faith.

> For by grace you have been saved through faith; and that not of yourselves, it is the gift of God; not as a result of works, so that no one may boast. (Ephesians 2:8–9)

We accept God's gift of salvation simply by placing our faith in Christ alone for the forgiveness of our sins. Would you like to enter a relationship with your Creator by trusting in Christ as your Savior? If so, here's a simple prayer you can use to express your faith:

> *Dear God,*
>
> *I know that my sin has put a barrier between You and me. Thank You for sending Your Son, Jesus, to die in my place. I trust in Jesus alone to forgive my sins, and I accept His gift of eternal life. I ask Jesus to be my personal Savior and the Lord of my life. Thank You. In Jesus's name, amen.*

If you've prayed this prayer or one like it and you wish to find out more about knowing God and His plan for you in the Bible, contact us at Insight for Living Ministries. Our contact information is on the following pages.

WE ARE HERE FOR YOU

If you desire to find out more about knowing God and His plan for you in the Bible, contact us. Insight for Living Ministries provides staff pastors who are available for free written correspondence or phone consultation. These seminary-trained and seasoned counselors have years of experience and are well-qualified guides for your spiritual journey.

Please feel welcome to contact your regional Pastoral Ministries by using the information below:

United States
Insight for Living
Pastoral Ministries
Post Office Box 269000
Plano, Texas 75026-9000
USA
972-473-5097, Monday through Friday,
8:00 a.m.–5:00 p.m. central time
www.insight.org/contactapastor

Canada
Insight for Living Canada
Pastoral Ministries
PO Box 8 Stn A
Abbotsford BC V2T 6Z4
CANADA
1-800-663-7639
info@insightforliving.ca

Australia, New Zealand, and South Pacific
Insight for Living Australia
Pastoral Care
Post Office Box 443
Boronia, VIC 3155
AUSTRALIA
1300 467 444

United Kingdom and Europe
Insight for Living United Kingdom
Pastoral Care
PO Box 553
Dorking
RH4 9EU
UNITED KINGDOM
0800 787 9364
+44 (0)1306 640156
pastoralcare@insightforliving.org.uk

ENDNOTES

1. Adapted from Wayne Stiles, *Going Places with God: A Devotional Journey Through the Lands of the Bible* (Ventura, Calif.: Regal, 2006), 26. Used by permission.

2. Adapted from Stiles, *Going Places with God*, 32. Used by permission.

3. Adapted from Stiles, *Going Places with God*, 47. Used by permission.

4. Adapted from Stiles, *Going Places with God*, 55. Used by permission.

5. Adapted from Stiles, *Going Places with God*, 65. Used by permission.

6. Adapted from Stiles, *Going Places with God*, 78. Used by permission.

7. Adapted from Stiles, *Going Places with God*, 83. Used by permission.

8. Adapted from Stiles, *Going Places with God*, 92. Used by permission.

9. Adapted from Stiles, *Going Places with God*, 134. Used by permission.

10. Adapted from Stiles, *Going Places with God*, 145. Used by permission.

11. Adapted from Stiles, *Going Places with God*, 111. Used by permission.

12. Adapted from Stiles, *Going Places with God*, 116. Used by permission.

13. Adapted from Stiles, *Going Places with God*, 125. Used by permission.

14. Adapted from Stiles, *Going Places with God*, 128. Used by permission.

15. Adapted from Stiles, *Going Places with God*, 146. Used by permission.

Resources for Probing Further

To further your study of the New Testament, we recommend the following resources. Of course, we cannot always endorse everything a writer or ministry says, so we encourage you to approach these and all other non-biblical resources with wisdom and discernment.

Bailey, Mark, and Tom Constable. *The New Testament Explorer: Discovering the Essence, Background, and Meaning of Every Book in the New Testament.* Nashville: Thomas Nelson, 1999.

Barker, Kenneth L., and John R. Kohlenberger III, eds. *The Expositor's Bible Commentary: New Testament.* Abridged ed. Grand Rapids: Zondervan, 2004.

Beitzel, Barry J. *The New Moody Atlas of the Bible.* Chicago: Moody Press, 2009.

Bruce, F. F. *New Testament History.* New York: Doubleday-Galilee, 1980.

House, H. Wayne. *Chronological and Background Charts of the New Testament.* 2nd. ed. Grand Rapids: Zondervan, 2009.

Jensen, Irving L. *Jensen's Survey of the New Testament.* Chicago: Moody Publishers, 1981.

Radmacher, Earl D., Ronald B. Allen, and H. W. House, eds. *Nelson's New Illustrated Bible Commentary: Spreading the Light of God's Word into Your Life.* Nashville: Thomas Nelson, 1999.

Tenney, Merril C., ed. *Zondervan's Pictorial Bible Dictionary*.
Grand Rapids: Zondervan, 1999.

Walvoord, John F., and Roy B. Zuck, eds. *The Bible Knowledge
Commentary: New Testament*. Wheaton, Ill.: Victor Books,
1989.

Wiersbe, Warren W. *The Wiersbe Bible Commentary:
New Testament*. Colorado Springs: David C. Cook, 2007.

Ordering Information

If you would like to order additional copies of *Insight's Bible Reading Guide: New Testament* or to order other Insight for Living Ministries resources, please contact the office that serves you.

United States

Insight for Living
Post Office Box 269000
Plano, Texas 75026-9000
USA
1-800-772-8888
(Monday through Friday, 7:00 a.m.–7:00 p.m. central time)
www.insight.org
www.insightworld.org

Canada

Insight for Living Canada
PO Box 8 Stn A
Abbottsford BC V2T 6Z4
CANADA
1-800-663-7639
www.insightforliving.ca

Australia, New Zealand, and South Pacific

Insight for Living Australia
Post Office Box 443
Boronia, VIC 3155
AUSTRALIA
1300 467 444
www.insight.asn.au

United Kingdom and Europe
Insight for Living United Kingdom
PO Box 553
Dorking
RH4 9EU
UNITED KINGDOM
0800 787 9364
www.insightforliving.org.uk

Other International Locations
International constituents may contact the U.S. office
through our Web site (www.insightworld.org), mail queries,
or by calling +1-972-473-5136.